Generation Shift

How generational evolution is changing the way we think, work and live

Eliza Filby

Contents

Chapter 3. Generations as Citizens

Acknowledgements

About the Author

As is the generation of leaves, so to of men:
At one time the wind shakes the leaves to the ground
but then the flourishing woods
Gives birth, and the season of spring comes
into existence;
So it is with the generations of men, which
alternately come forth and pass away.

Homer, the *Illiad*, Book Six

'I think time and family are part of the same thing really; the generation is the actual unit of time by which humanity lives.'

James Meek

Introduction

Generation Shift is an edited collection of my essays written between the onset of the pandemic in 2020, and the summer of 2023. The earlier works reflect a time when the consequences of that huge disruption were just beginning to be felt in our workplaces, wallets, and in society. Later articles build on that work and are drawn from my experiences advising companies and institutions all over the world on generational change.

The pandemic triggered a monumental shift in more ways than one. Firstly, and most obviously, it triggered a revolution in work – or at least in office work. Throughout the first lockdown I conducted a series of interviews with various professions, from Uber drivers to wedding planners and from investment managers to accountants, and one thing stood out above all; the extent to which everyone (even those still leaving the house for work) were enjoying the change of pace and greater autonomy over their time. I have written several pieces on the future of work and this collection shows the evolution of my thinking.

Secondly, the pandemic symbolised a generational shift in society. Gen Zers raised their voices effectively for the first time; mocking millennials who were now hitting mid-life and giving clarity to a fresh perspective on the world. Boomers, too, were made to feel vulnerable for the first time, which triggered a change in their dominant position in society as a result. Thirdly, and perhaps most pressingly, is our changing position as consumers in the twenty-first century; not just as a result of being locked inside our homes but also due to the uncertain economic climate that followed the pandemic.

There are, of course, huge challenges with segmenting society by age but in an era of such major disruption, understanding how life cycles are changing, how different generations are evolving and emerging, and how the family unit is strengthening is, I believe, a worthwhile exercise.

We hear so much about technological and political disruption, but what I've attempted to do here is explain 'human disruption' – the different ways that we are now living our lives and how that is defining the twenty-first century. Happy reading!

Eliza

Chapter 1:
Generations and the Future of Work

1. Why We Are All Tired of Our Jobs
(*UnHerd*, 13 May 2020)

Even before Covid-19 struck, 'lifestyle' work was losing its lustre.
Now it's dead and buried

When the British Government imposed a three-day working week during the oil crisis in 1973, many economists expected a productivity drop of at least forty per cent. It didn't happen. People adjusted, worked harder, and became more efficient. In the end, even though people were in work less, they were working more.

Fast-forward fifty years and the situation today has triggered an equally huge adjustment in our work patterns. All workers have had specific challenges, whether it's the key worker whose status has risen and whose workload has increased (but whose pay and conditions have not) or the managerial class now working from home, tag-teaming childcare commitments with partners, and struggling with the virtual office.

One obvious characteristic of this pandemic experience is that we have a renewed sense of what is *valuable* work in society: saluting farmers, supermarket workers, bin men, and delivery drivers. Health and care workers have been elevated beyond a workforce to the status of a sacrificial army for their undeniable duty and bravery. We do not wear poppies to show our respect but clap in the street to show our thanks. There is a new appreciation for schools, too, not just for their role in educating kids but as wrap-around childcare that enables parents to work. And how many other informal paid workers, from cleaners to childminders, do we now realise are fundamental to making our households — and our economy — tick?

This is an important corrective to the past two decades, which were characterised by a steady decline in respect, status, and stability for jobs categorised as 'low-skilled'. Associated with debates around immigration, education, and inequality, the issue has dogged politics in most countries for years and has been both ignition and accelerant to the populist flame.

But as well as reminding us of underappreciated but vital roles, the pandemic has also made us think about the purpose of work at the other end of the social scale. Before Covid, a Gallup poll found that eighty-seven per cent of workers in the UK felt disengaged in their job[1], and it is doubtful whether this figure would improve today just because so many of us are working from home.

How many workers are discovering how little they actually do in the office (and that it can be done at home in half the time)? Or perhaps workers are finding the exact opposite; things that used to take ten minutes in the office now take an hour over Zoom. Kids are exposed to what Mummy and Daddy call 'work' — lots of time looking at a screen; something we berate them for doing too much of and an activity that is hardly inspiring for them to see. How many workers are waking up to the fact that the rhythms and responsibilities that defined them aren't as necessary or as important as they thought?

Given the economic slump that will follow this pandemic, it is unlikely that we will see a mass of dissatisfied workers walking out of their jobs; most will seek stability rather than change. But, even if this lockdown experience is not leading us to question our careers, it is undoubtedly making us question our record on work/life balance. There are three reasons to work: financial survival, professional and financial status, and personal meaning and identity. Since the nineties, especially among the graduate class, it was the latter that was encouraged. A *career* was increasingly where individuals found their purpose. Finding the 'right' fit became a full-time pursuit, consuming all spare hours, weekends, and most of our twenties. If we took a wrong turn, we labelled it a quarter-life crisis and simply trained for something else.

Nowhere was this more encouraged than in the millennial generation, whose educational and parenting culture was entirely CV-driven. And for the first time in history, it was a gender-neutral pursuit, with millennial women being instructed that finding the right career was far more important than finding the right partner.

The ultimate status update for millennials was not to be in love but to be in love with your job.

By the mid-noughties, just as manual labour declined and was increasingly dismissed by an educational establishment, we began to romanticise self-actualisation through work. Out went the slacker trends of the nineties: the dead-end jobs, artistic fantasies, faint-hearted careers, and twentysomethings slumped on the sofa as in *Friends*. Rents became too high, tuition fees had to be paid back, and a global recession was looming. Work became the ultimate realising of the self. It was not the music we liked or the hobbies we pursued, but our careers that gave us our uniform, self-meaning, and network.

Tech idealists were the chief evangelists of this rewriting of the Protestant work ethic, with Steve Jobs the guiding prophet, immortalised by an unwillingness to compromise, global success, and premature death: 'Your time is limited, so don't waste it living someone else's life . . . have the courage to follow your heart and intuition.'

Where we worked and where we wanted to work began to reflect this new culture. Again, the pioneers were the dotcoms of the early noughties and their influence signified what may be called the 'Californication of the office'; evident today in even the dullest of corporate places. It became a space designed not for monotonous, uninspiring work but for constant play with breakout zones, super-slides, free-breakfast bars, gyms, and sleep pods. As a casino is designed to keep out daylight, so these offices are engineered to make you feel like you are not at work at all (and to keep you there for as long as possible).

Work benefits began to reflect these new priorities. Out went gold-plated pensions (a route map to eventual departure) and in came very different perks, from pet insurance to unpaid sabbaticals, even an egg-freezing service[2] and a breast milk courier system[3].

WeWork was the apotheosis of this trend. In the words of its poster-boy founder, Adam Neumann, WeWork was where people 'made a life not just a living' and whose spaces were based on 'mission and fulfilment — not only salary'. WeWork's mission was always more impressive than its finances[4]. Co-working spaces reflected the lionising of the lone, disruptive entrepreneur — even though the majority of WeWork's clients were large corporations seeking to tap into the zeitgeist. The original concept of WeWork as a commune was always fantastical: there was no 'we' in WeWork; it reflected the decades-long breakdown of the employer-employee relationship.

It was not surprising that in this exhaustive search for meaning and purpose we were becoming exhausted. Work seeped into our weekends, our social events, and ultimately into our homes — especially as the global recession hit and wages fell. We monetised our hobbies through side-hustles and further allowed the intrusion of work into our leisure time. The millennial generation in particular, far from their lazy, entitled stereotype, were becoming 'work martyrs', more likely than any other generation to answer emails at the weekends.

But then came the Great Pause: Covid-19. No company, individual, or government could have engineered that experiment if they'd tried. It is a real test of an employer's obligations to their workforce. It is a real test of how accommodating employers are to workers' work/life balance and familial responsibilities. It is a real test for workers as to whether they actually enjoy their jobs and how fulfilling they find them. I am currently conducting a series of lockdown interviews with different professions, from CEOs to yoga teachers, and it is striking how little people are talking about work and how much they are talking about renewed fulfilment in the family, hobbies, and home. Is this the time when we stop pretending we love our jobs?

They say it takes sixty-six days to build a new habit[5], and given some of the predictions of how long it will take to get back to normality, some are starting to think that it will never happen — certainly not in the workplace. A recent Ipsos MORI poll found that seventy-five per cent of Britons expect their work-life balance to change because of Covid-19[6]. The question is *how*? Certainly, those workers — mostly parents — who have had to fight with their companies for flexible working will never have to make the case again. Even two-week paternity leave now seems woefully inadequate.

Even after social distancing ends, companies may find that they will have to justify why workers need to be in the office at all. With more remote working and staggered shifts, loyalty and camaraderie among workers will become a problem especially for new entrants. Some are already experimenting with all sorts of virtual bonding, from cocktail lessons to quiz nights — but is this really comparable to a quick drink before the commuter train?

Even when lockdown is lifted and with social distancing measures still in operation, the office will be a very different place. Out go sleep pods (unhygienic) and breakout zones (too social); maybe cubicles will once again become the norm?

More pointedly, many companies and organisations, especially in a recession, will use this change as an excuse to 'shave off some of the fat', with many roles, departments, and people now considered surplus to requirements. Businesses are already sniffing out the huge savings to be made in reducing leased office space. It may be that office HQ becomes like a church: a place for regular worship, a sermon, communion, and the odd study class, but with staggered service times and empty most of the time. The expectation will be that the majority of individuals' work is performed outside the building.

But if true, consider the ramifications for those dependent on a thriving office community in our cities: from sandwich shops to cleaners to transport infrastructure. Business districts on a Sunday are ghost towns — do we really want that to become the quotidian norm? And what of the ramifications for company culture? Will the diversity deficit, 'mansplaining', and even sexual harassment no longer be features of working life or will these problems only intensify or be ignored in a working world dominated by Zoom? The suggested model published by the Adam Smith Institute last week of 'four days in work, ten days at home'[7] may, depending on how long it lasts, totally destroy the concept of a weekend and put us all on a rota rhythm that may feel more disruptive than lockdown itself.

All these changes will be for the corporate class, of course, or at least the office class. And big business will adapt much more slowly than nimbler, smaller outfits. The self-employed already have much of this flexibility built-in, but they may find that with fewer people in the office their services are needed less, and so become the easiest to discard. There is already a divide between workers; those who can work from home and those who can't — and that divide will only intensify post-Covid.

During this pandemic, all those things that are not usually recognised in the economy, such as care and cleaning (typically female jobs) are now what the economy hinges upon. The professional classes, currently leaning out of their windows to clap on a Thursday night, will soon find themselves confronted by a new world of work, but will this lead to a new era of work/life balance? Probably not: all the research suggests that a clear divide between personal and professional boundaries in life results in greater happiness.

So, before we all rip off our lanyards in liberation, it is important to consider how the blurring of boundaries that comes with more remote flexible working may backfire; meaning in fact that we are all working harder, longer, and more often. It is surely time to stop pretending that it is the key thing that defines us.

2. Why We All May Regret the Remote Revolution
(*Daily Mail*, 15 July 2020)

When the Government imposed a three-day working week during the 1973 oil crisis, it feared a productivity drop of at least forty per cent. That didn't happen. In the end, even though people spent less time in their workplace, they made up for it by working more efficiently and at home. Fast-forward almost fifty years and the coronavirus pandemic — 'the Great Pause', as it has been dubbed – triggered an equally huge adjustment in work patterns worldwide.

Before lockdown was introduced back in March 2020, millions of workers would have laughed in disbelief if you told them that throughout that period they would be working from the confines of their home. And yet, forty-nine per cent of the British workforce was doing just that in some form, according to the Office for National Statistics (ONS)[8]. In June, just under one-third of US workers teleworked or worked from home[9] and in France, remote working more than doubled compared to one year before, increasing by twenty-five percentage points[10]. When you factor in Britain's 9.1 million furloughed workers — who are excluded from the data — that figure is even more staggering.

So it's hardly surprising that when the then PM Boris Johnson suggested that 'people should start to think about getting back to work', his comment was met with a collective groan. According to a survey carried out for the Business Clean Air Taskforce, nine out of ten Britons who've worked from home would like to continue to do so to some degree after restrictions are fully lifted[11].

Even business behemoths such as Barclays — which, in the words of CEO Jes Staley, has been run 'by people in their own kitchens' during lockdown — are now evaluating the need for a 7,000-capacity office, while Whitehall is manned by only a skeleton staff of civil servants in situ. Twitter staff worldwide have been told they can work remotely indefinitely and Mark Zuckerberg has suggested that half of Facebook's 45,000 employees will work from home within a decade.

Many companies are already sniffing out the huge financial savings to be made in reducing leased office space. After all, a single desk in some prime London locations can cost up to £60,000 a year. This will, of course, have huge ramifications for those dependent on a thriving office community in our cities.

Sandwich delis remain shut, coffee shops are closed, and entire business hubs now resemble desolate ghost towns. Meanwhile, with trains and buses still empty, revenue gained from our transport infrastructure has all but ground to a halt. It was hardly surprising the ONS reported the UK economy had dropped by a quarter since February before the lockdown and grew by only 1.8 per cent in May[12].

It's clear that any hope of a so-called 'V-shaped' recovery depends on Britain getting back to work immediately. But the economic devastation of working from home (WFH) is only one aspect of its concerning impact on society.

Indeed, as well as being bad for the economy I fear that, rather than liberating us, it is also making us more miserable and enslaved to our work lives than ever. And ultimately that is why our workforce must return to the office as soon as it can. Of course, that isn't to say that working from home doesn't have its advantages.

The pandemic has given many people much needed time to consider the real purpose of work. Before Covid-19 came along, analytics firm Gallup found eighty-seven per cent of workers in the UK felt disengaged in their job[13]. But now that these workers are no longer confined to the office, how many are discovering how little they actually do on a day-to-day basis — and that it can be done at home in half the time?

Certainly, there is a ruthless efficiency about working from home: without a daily commute, you can be at your desk earlier and plough on later, all with less distraction.

But these benefits come at a heavy price: the end of the work/life balance.

No longer able to end their workday by leaving the office, I suspect many employees now working remotely find it increasingly hard to 'clock off' when their normal working day ends — according to one survey, forty-four per cent say they 'struggle to switch off'[14]. And even with the best intentions, on a physical level the boundaries between your office and living space soon become blurred — all it takes is a phone call or online message for you to be dragged back to your virtual desk.

Some bosses are already thinking ahead about the dramatic change in how and where we work. Just last month, Arjun Kaicker, head of analytics and insights at the multinational firm Zaha Hadid Architects, suggested offices may soon 'evolve into something much more [like] a clubhouse'. 'A lot of companies have a great staff gym or have fantastic subsidised or free food and they'll have come for that and not necessarily to even work,' he said[15]. If true, and workers do one day go 'into the office' not to do any work at all, but with the sole purpose of pursuing leisure and socialising, the destruction of our work/life balance will be complete. That need for social interaction should not be underestimated. Around half of lockdown homeworkers report feeling more isolated[16].

Some companies are trying to tackle the problem by experimenting with all sorts of virtual bonding, from cocktail lessons to quiz nights. But is this really comparable to grabbing a lunchtime sandwich in a cafe with a colleague or quick drink before the commuter train home?

It is becoming clear WFH may only be the start of even more drastic changes. Take one study by Imperial College London, which suggested companies should now operate on a model of four days in work, ten days at home[17]. But such a regime would completely destroy the concept of the 'week-weekend' model that is ingrained in us as much as the seasons.

And so before we all rip off our lanyards in liberation, before we decide the great WFH debate is already settled, we must beware that we could end up working harder, longer, more often — and feeling ever more isolated.

In such a scenario we risk losing the very things that make us human.

3. Why WFH May Not Be Good for Women
(*City A.M.*, 14 August 2021)

Cabinet ministers and CEOs are falling over themselves trying to bark us back into the office. Some are even threatening to cut our pay if we move too far away, but their sledgehammer approach is not winning converts, especially among women. Over the course of sixteen months of remote working, many of us have felt liberated from our heels, bras, and even unwanted wandering hands. Remote working in a pandemic may have brought as many pressures as freedoms, but there is no doubt that women in particular favour a flexible future.

Women feel remote working makes them better workers, according to data from the Office of National Statistics[18]. Other surveys have pointed to women's growing view of flexibility **as a dealbreaker in employment conditions**[19]. Remote working has been accompanied with a desire for remote living (which will probably continue even if companies do decrease wages for those fully on-line workers). It's been predicted that **more than 300,000 Londoners** could migrate over the next year, with the capital's population likely to fall for the first time in thirty years[20] – driven by those with families seeking more space and flexibility.

In those pre-pandemic days, city living was associated with cosmopolitanism, convenience, and opportunity. But after a couple of weeks of lockdown, proximity to green space and a decent amount of square footage trumped all those pop-up restaurants, coffee shops, and galleries that remained closed.

So the great migration and remote working experiment is under way, but are women – and working mothers in particular – wise to embrace it so readily?

Our generation's escape from the Big Smoke is very different to our parents' experience back in the eighties, primarily because the economic makeup of households is now more complex. Forget male-only breadwinners; **the majority of millennial couples are dual earners** – the largest percentage ever – and seventy-one per cent of mothers now work[21]. Over the last eighteen months this has meant (in our house at least) a tussle over who gets the most comfortable chair and desk, how childcare is divvied up, and who makes the dinner. Even the most progressive marriages struggle with the debate over whose career should take precedence and often it comes down to who earns the most. For decades, women have played out this fight in the workplace and now, however healthy their partnership is, many are having to fight for this right in the home.

In this new era, we can forget those outdated visions of Stepford Wives and 'keeping up with the Joneses': the twenty-first century, remote-working mother won't have time. Millennial men may have stepped up in terms of housework and childcare compared to their predecessors, but the burden for most of these responsibilities has fallen, and will continue to fall disproportionately, on women[22]. If you are used to the convenience and support structures of the city, rural living can come as a real shock. Paid and affordable help, something that working women have increasingly relied on over the last twenty years, is much harder to find the more remote you are. No wonder many families are choosing to live near grandparents. However we frame it, remote working puts women back in the home – albeit in front of a Zoom screen rather than the kitchen sink.

Cities have always been associated with fear and frustration for women – as the tragic murder of Sarah Everard and the ensuing debate about female safety revealed. But let's not forget that cities have also been a place for female freedom, opportunity, and expression, too. Back in the noughties, *Sex and the City* encapsulated the excitement of a new generation of professional women roaming city streets, free from the social constraints and etiquette of earlier times. Where Carrie Bradshaw led, so Lena Dunham, Phoebe Waller-Bridge, Michaela Coel, and Aisling Bea have followed, documenting in unfiltered honesty women's love affair with the urban playground and giving a two-fingered salute to all the frustrated suburban housewives that dominated the sitcoms of yesteryear.

But let's not pretend cities, especially London, are easy places for families. The microaggressions you experience with a pram on public transport are enough to make you literally run for the hills. And that's before you even start thinking about school places and property prices. There is evidence however that city-dwelling may be better for your marriage. Eight of the ten local authorities with the lowest divorce rates are in London, followed by Oxford and Cambridge, whereas Hastings, now being pitched as Britain's best commuter seaside town, has the second highest proportion of divorced people in the country[23].

The real danger of course is that while flexible working undoubtedly makes childcare easier, it will make female promotion less likely, placing at risk all the hard work that women have put in over the last forty years. Stanford academic and remote-working expert, Nicholas Bloom, has summarised the challenge for companies: 'My biggest fear is all the single young men come in five days a week, and college-educated women with a six-year-old and an eight-year-old come in two days a week, and six to seven years down the road there's a huge difference in promotion rates and you have a diversity crisis.'[24]

To avoid this, companies will need policies in place to ensure a culture of presenteeism doesn't hold, in part by incentivising those who are always in to stay at home and those who mostly work from home to come in. According to an ONS survey, women feel that while working from home prevented them from 'thinking outside the box'[25] it also made them more efficient workers, whereas men considered that homeworking aided their creativity and self-care. Try satisfying all those urges rather than tampering with pay scales if you want to keep hold of your best talent.

And yet the domestic shift needed is an even bigger challenge than the corporate one. If the twentieth century saw the rise of the professional female, so the twenty-first century must give birth to the domesticated male, especially if this new hybrid working is going to work equally for dual-income couples. Good intentions are not enough: we need policies and financial incentives if we are to normalise the sight of a man carrying a baby in a sling as much as we have normalised a woman on a commuter train.

Evidence from the US suggests we are a long way off; millennial men are actually more conservative than their predecessors. Sharing her research on dual-income couples in the *Harvard Business Review*, Avivah Wittenberg Cox has concluded that while many high-profile men are 'happy to have successful, high-earning wives' and 'applaud and support them', they do so only 'until it starts to interfere with their own careers'. She found that wives were under the misconception that 'well-educated couples would be mutually supportive and take turns, helping each other become all they can be' and found themselves shocked at the reality. Wittenberg Cox's advice to professional females is rather blunt: 'If you can't find a spouse who supports your career, stay single.'[26]

Women should remember that although those office heels may have pinched our feet, at least we were liberated from the apron strings. Women have come too far, and the city has too much to offer for us (even working mums) to abandon it completely. But the fact is that if hybrid working is the future then this can only be fully realised if hybrid households become the norm as well.

4. How the Rise of Entrepreneur Culture Explains the Great Resignation
(8 March 2022)

Entrepreneurialism is the new rock 'n' roll so is it any wonder that being on the corporate conveyor belt has lost its appeal?

Review of *Diary of a CEO Live*, London Palladium, 22 February 2022

The London Palladium's corridors are filled with mementos of yesterday's headliners, from Frank Sinatra to Lloyd Webber musicals, and yet the audience this evening is not here for distraction from their daily lives, but for inspiration; an altogether different kind of stardust. It is probably the most diverse audience that the Palladium has ever seen, all eagerly awaiting rock star entrepreneur Steven Bartlett, founder of a multi-million-pound listed company and now the host of the UK's No.1 podcast, *Diary of a CEO*. He's also the youngest ever 'dragon' on BBC1's *Dragon's Den*.

Bartlett walks onto the stage, dressed in black jeans and a T-shirt, and takes a seat with his infamous diary in hand. He deliberately projects an everyman image, and in many ways is a poster boy for our times. Forget *Love Island*, the Instafamous, and airbrushed perfectionism – Bartlett is a new type of influencer: a teacher, a sage, an accessible big brother who inspires action, not envy. As the young crowd claps, roars, and leaps to their feet, swaying to the gospel choir that accompanies his life story, they become followers in the truest sense of the word.

Bartlett's story as a working-class bi-racial kid from a predominantly white town is one of struggle and structural racism, but also of self-discovery. His journey – from college dropout to social media millionaire – is a modern pilgrim's progress full of temptation, sacrifice, and eventual enlightenment. Bartlett's yet another college quitter who scaled the heights of unimaginable success; a fact that undoubtedly resonated with the young audience for whom tertiary education is no longer a guaranteed path to social mobility but more the road to debt.

Bartlett's allure lies not just in his story but also in his ability to quit. In 2019, he took his company, Social Chain, public on the Dusseldorf Stock Exchange – the pinnacle for any founder – but left a year later. 'Quitting is for winners' he once tweeted, in one of his many bite-sized philosophical musings. 'Knowing when to quit, change direction . . . demand more from life, give up on something . . . is a very important skill that people who win at life all seem to have.' It was a tweet that would have spoken to anyone who has just endured two years on Zoom in a job they hated.

Steven Bartlett's precise appeal however lies in his twenty-first-century definition of success. *Happy Sexy Millionaire* is the title of his best-selling autobiography, and it is meant to be ironic. For Bartlett, happiness is found not in hot girls, Lamborghinis, and dollar signs, but in sincerity and humility. And his stage show is a re-telling of that story, packaged so that it applies to us all. He says little about how he built his business or led his team; instead we hear how he discovered true empathy and conquered his ego. He's the Dalai Lama crossed with Tony Robbins. His message is a deliberate antidote to the eighties materialism of our childhood and the tech-bro culture of yesteryear, and flies in the face of today's one-click consumption. And yet this is an overwhelmingly individualistic philosophy: forget structural obstacles, the only obstacle to your happiness is yourself, Bartlett preaches. He struts around the stage, urging us all to appreciate that 'validation is an inside job' and our goal is to 'follow our passion'.

Why is all this important? Well, because Bartlett's message, whether intentionally so or not, is one that captures the post-pandemic burnout mood, and one that is fuelling the Great Resignation. Put simply, it is a philosophy that all companies should be terrified of. There are many, of course, who dispute whether the Great Resignation exists, but ask anyone hiring right now and they will tell you recruitment and retention have never been harder. Legal firms are reportedly offering £150k starting salaries[27]. And on an anecdotal level, I spoke to one financial services company that is struggling to even train their first-class graduates, who are completely disengaged with their jobs. I've heard of agencies extending the search for talent to South Africa because they cannot fill roles in the UK and there is no time difference to complicate working days. Another HR director told me (only partly in jest), 'You wouldn't believe how many people have left us to start cupcake businesses.'

Anyone hiring these days should get off LinkedIn and start with Reddit's #antiwork thread or #greatresignation on TikTok to get a sense of how young people are talking and being educated about work. Grad schemes are no longer the golden ticket, but now a prison from which many feel they need to escape. Who can blame them? Many of those in corporate jobs have spent the last two years staring at a green dot and working not from the comfort of a home office, but in their bedrooms, and quite often from their beds. And staying in the same job with flexible working as a sweetener is not the answer. In between Zooms (or maybe during), your young recruits are scrolling their Insta stories and up will pop Steven Bartlett, this generation's John Lennon, telling them 'all you need is you' and to imagine a life that is better.

We are living in the age of hyper-individualism, a force that originated in the sixties and has reached its zenith today, fuelled by over-parenting, an individualistic and high-pressured education system, comparison culture, and personalised technology. It is an insurmountable force. Put bluntly, your well-intentioned and well-thought-out corporate values on your website are competing with the individualistic identities of kids who have been building their brand and 'net-rep' since they were in their early teens. And this is why maverick entrepreneurs such as Bartlett are today's sages; for the way they embody (unlike any organisation) that need for autonomy, building something that reflects their values, and the quest and excitement of embarking on a journey of self-fulfilment.

So what can companies do to counter the Bartlett philosophy? Nothing – they need to embrace it instead, by creating workplaces that allow the individual to thrive through creative self-expression and personalised learning, allowing their full identities to be realised in an environment that actually offers them the security and support they wouldn't have if they chanced it alone. That's easier said than done of course, but in an age of automation it has never been more possible and more economical to allow humans to do what they do best, and let machines do the rest.

5. The Rise of the Corporate Dad
(Published: 3 May 2022)

Back in 2017, long before live events were forced to retreat online, a childcare crisis in our household meant that my husband was forced to take our sleeping eight-month-old to a conference he was speaking at. The pram was parked near the stage and all was well until, midway through, our son woke up. My husband left the stage, scooped him out of the pram and fed him a bottle while bouncing him on his knee and resuming his speech. I subsequently heard from several people in that room, both male and female, that they considered the scene to be rather inspirational.

Had it been me on that stage, holding a baby while addressing the audience, the experience would have been very different. I would have scrambled around for the bottle, probably split the milk, apologised profusely to the audience and undoubtedly cut the event short. But my personal paranoia aside, I am also aware that different standards apply. Any sight of a mother with her baby in a work environment (in person or on Zoom) comes with the unscripted assumption that she is failing at her dual responsibilities. My husband, in contrast, on that day at least, was lauded for nailing his work/life balance and representing the very model of a modern man.

That my husband's public demonstration of fatherhood was greeted so admiringly by a business audience is small evidence of a quiet revolution that has gradually taken place in our workplaces and society at large. A new, positive culture of fatherhood now prevails. This is evident in the boardroom as much as at the school gates; evident in those centrist dads in their fifties in trainers doing their flipkicks at the skatepark with their offspring; evident in the multi-tasking millennial dad jogging with the Bugaboo on the nursery run while taking a work call on his ear pods; and evident in that beacon of modern masculinity, David Beckham, who has seemingly traded in football for fatherhood and whose pictures of daddy-daughter time inspire reams of columns.

In truth, a positive portrayal of fatherhood has been a long time coming. Gone are outdated Hollywood depictions of negligent, unresponsive, workaholic fathers omnipresent in eighties films, which served as cultural critiques of Reaganomics. Gone too are the clumsy TV ads of dads scorching the kids' dinner and ending up at McDonald's. And gone, thankfully, are the derogatory visions of male absenteeism, especially of black fathers. Modern, diverse fatherhood in the twenty-first century is arguably more positively portrayed than motherhood, particularly on social media. While the weird stratosphere of mummy-influencers eats itself with its faux-authenticity and ever-present bitchiness, dads have found comfort in the light-hearted and the anecdotal, with content such as the Parenting Hell podcast with Rob Beckett and Josh Widdicombe topping the charts. It's obvious which breeds greater solidarity.

An ad for Philadelphia cheese showing two fathers leaving a baby on a restaurant conveyor belt was banned in 2019 under new UK gender-stereotyping regulations.

This elevation of fatherhood though is part of a broader tale of the feminisation of men (and its ensuing commercialisation). Male grooming, wellness, self-help; modern masculinity is now an industry. Liquid lunches come in the form of Huel for the twenty-first century male, which as far as I can tell is the dry dust women have been dieting on for years but repackaged for the 'time-short, health-conscious man'.

Fatherhood, though, adds a comforting, humane layer to the culture of self-optimisation. So the millennial father speaks not of his 4 a.m. fitness routine but of midnight nappy changes and cures for colic; talks not of his mindfulness meditation but of being 'present' with his kids in the park. Because in fatherhood, men have found the tonic they've been looking for, the necessary dilution to toxic masculinity. In an age of labels, being a father gives the heteronormative male desirable distinction, a standout quality, and even more so when he's the father of a girl. He talks with vested interest and genuine concern about smashing the patriarchy (albeit in a patrician tone).

But more than that, fatherhood has become the chief way that men, especially older men in power, seek a common language with women (seemingly of any age or description) in the workplace. As the boss shares his screensaver of his delightful offspring and regales you with stories of sleepless nights and spelling tests, the subtext is clear: 'I'm not a creep'. This is what makes for workplace gender relations in the post #MeToo era. But more than that, fatherhood is the male workers' superpower. Men have benefitted from parenthood in the workplace but without the struggle and the sacrifice that befalls women. Working fathers are more likely to be promoted than childless men or childless women and, of course, working mothers[28]. You will hear CEO fathers speak (without irony) of how parenthood has made them a better leader. 'As a father you have to be a role model, an example, a good listener, a visionary, one who can encourage, one who creates accountability, and one who problem solves,' said one US CEO in an interview with Inc., adding, 'I've learned that all the attributes necessary to be a successful father are equally important to being a successful business leader.'[29] Never mind the fact that many CEOs have stay-at-home wives or that, according to one study of Danish firms, male CEOs actually paid their employees less generously after fathering a child[30]. The more serious point is that these skills were never (and are still not) acknowledged or valued for working mothers. Unsurprisingly, female CEOs are less likely to have children than their male counterparts[31].

We need not dig too deep to discover why the birth rate is in decline and more and more women are choosing to be child-free. The story over the past thirty years is of women having better options and more freedom, but that juggling those choices with children has become next to impossible.

In many respects, millennial women are heading for greater mid-life frustration than their forebears, having been sold a false promise of an egalitarian marriage and a more equal world, still stung by the pregnancy penalty and with the frightening prospect of having to undertake most of the care in an ageing society with inadequate state social care support. We all knew that the equality narrative we were fed as young women was tosh but it has been sharply revealed by this pandemic. While most of my dad friends all spoke of the joy of additional 'quality' time with their kids over lockdown, my mother friends spoke of a very different war: one of insurmountable juggling and fighting for the mental space and very often the physical space to work. Around 1.4 million of US mothers have quit the workplace since the start of the pandemic[32]. *The New York Times* even set up a Primal Scream hotline so that mothers could scream their frustrations down the phone[33].

My aim is not to degrade fathers: I was raised by a stay-at-home dad (very avant-garde in the eighties) and my husband mucks in more than anyone I know. However, we should not exaggerate the progress made; paternity leave take-up rates are appalling, while no marriage I know has equality in the domestic sphere. Fatherhood may be entering a new, positive phase and fathers have definitely stepped up, but perhaps we should be questioning how we can move it forward to better supporting mothers, particularly in the workplace where the mood is ripe for change. When an expectant father announces with a gleeful expression, 'We're having a baby!' I want scream and say, 'There's no *we* about it, mate'. The new fetishisation of fatherhood is certainly a sign of progress, but let's not pretend that we're on a road to genuine equality – either in the workplace or the home.

6. Why the Future of Work Lies in the Hands of Each Company
(Published: 14 July 2022)

As the ripples of lockdown and troubles in the economy continue to shape the future of the work debate, the emerging consensus is that there is no consensus, and each company is finding its own path

Over the past six weeks I've spoken to CEOs, partners, HR leaders, specialists, and trainers in sectors ranging from investment banking to agritech, from mortgage brokers to lawyers, across the US, EU, India, the Middle East, and the UK, representing everything from multinationals to local companies, with employee numbers ranging from 100 to 10,000. They are still reeling from the fallout from the pandemic – the Great Resignation, worker burnout, and the shift to flexible working – and all, to varying degrees, are now faced with the cost-of-living crisis and a troubled world economy.

The predominant feeling is one of insecurity. Many are tiptoeing in the dark, testing policies and approaches, the consequences and effectiveness of which will only be realised in three to five years' time. Here are my five observations on where the 'future of work' debate currently stands.

1. The Worker Revolution is Unequal
The Covid lockdown mandated an already well-entrenched divide between those who could work from home and those who could not. Post-pandemic, this crude demarcation between white collar and blue-collar workers has only intensified, and it has worrying consequences. We know that when people talk about 'the future of work' what they are really referring to is knowledge workers. It was telling that during the recent rail strikes in the UK, the unions chose to strike on Tuesday, Thursday, and Saturday, the most disruptive days in the new hybrid era, with weekend chaos thrown in for good measure.

It's an observation that points to a bigger truth in the UK, that the fate of the railway infrastructure is no longer inextricably linked to knowledge workers on the constant commute. Transport is just one of many sectors and businesses that once relied on the commuter class and has been forced to adapt (or strike) to survive. You only need to take a brief walk around once-bustling business districts to see the now boarded-up victims of the hybrid revolution, from dry cleaners to cafes. The economic interests of blue- and white-collar workers are now not only dislocated but, in some instances, are also in direct conflict. In truth, there is a growing inequality between white collar and blue-collar workers' rights and fate, evidenced in the difference in causes, methods, and even the language used to differentiate between the two statuses. For those businesses with both types of workers (indeed any with cleaners and receptionists), the challenge of how to serve the interests of all their workers in an equitable way will become ever more difficult.

But of course, inequality is very evident *within* the white-collar classes too. As one senior executive confessed to me, there were several of his staff who, he knew, had insufficient stability to endure a prolonged financial squeeze. Impromptu 'salary top-ups' for employees is one strategy being deployed by many companies to ease the immediate difficulties. But, as the recession hits and employees feel the ever-increasing pinch, expect more and more companies to reprioritise from mental wellbeing to financial wellbeing. This is all well-intentioned, but workers themselves might reasonably begin to prioritise stability and salary more than ever.

2. The Knowledge Worker Revolution is One of Values not Just Logistics

Billionaire Elon Musk and Tory MP Jacob Rees Mogg have little in common, but both are willing to say in public what many leaders and CEOs are only willing to say in private; that everyone should just get back into the office. Indeed, one CEO confessed to me his hope that the recession would scare his employees into compliance. But the opposite may be the case. In an era of rising inflation, employees may argue that the cost of commuting is something they could do without.

But all this conceals a fundamental truth that all CEOs must understand: the knowledge worker revolution has never just been about location and logistics but a more profound desire for greater autonomy. To an unprecedented degree, the pandemic gave us time; time to think about the role of work and its place in our lives after decades of a business culture that tried to force corporate purpose into our individual identities. Unsurprisingly, Gen Zers – who grew up with the world's knowledge in their pockets and who have been building their brand since they were in their early teens – are the ones least likely to subscribe to this philosophy. They tend to ask not only what they can do for their employer but also what their employer can do for them. They are also the ones for whom multiple streams of revenue makes perfect sense, rather than one fixed salary. Such attitudes can leave older workers perplexed, but also inspired.

What is clear is that countless companies are mistakenly focusing on the logistics of the hybrid model by setting in stone a policy of flexible working (which is inherently inflexible) while ignoring the underlying call for greater worker autonomy. For some, the pandemic granted them the gift of time to reorder their relationship with their families, health, homes, and wealth. For others, it was an intense two years of hyper-productivity and loose boundaries, resulting in complete burnout. Whatever the employees' experience, it fundamentally made us think about what we do and how we work. What workers want, therefore, is not a set number of days stipulated for an appearance in the office, but to have greater control over their time, over the kind of work they are doing, how they are being managed, and what they learn. It is no good telling Gen Z they have to learn the ropes; there has to be a sense of FOMO created around the office and that learning has to be bespoke, highly engaging, and well managed. The age of deference to the office and to the hierarchical structures embodied in office buildings is over.

The companies that get hybrid work right will be the ones who think beyond the logistics and instead see it for what it is: a fundamental rewriting of the social contract between employer and employee. Meaningless corporate values on your website no longer cut it.

3. The Knowledge Worker Revolution Rests on Managers Not Leaders

'Leaders eat last' wrote guru Simon Sinek,[34] and in many respects that message has never been more important if CEOs and senior executives want to demonstrate the kind of authenticity, democracy, and transparency that employees now expect in the post-pandemic workplace. But in the hybrid world, it is managers, not leaders, who are the real key to its success. The most impressive hybrid policies I have witnessed have been completely localised and autonomously governed by managers within small teams. These are truly flexible policies that change from week to week, depending on projects and workload. They consider everyone's domestic set-up and don't just favour parents. The more experienced recognise their face-to-face obligations to the young, while the young feel heard and enthused. At the root is the sense of duty and reciprocal responsibility to each other that is the foundation of belonging to any organisation.

4. The Knowledge Worker Revolution Is Ageist

It is understandable why companies currently seem obsessed with enticing and retaining Gen Z in the age of the Great Resignation. The truth is that young people are cheap and older workers are expensive. The untold story of the Great Resignation, though, is the Grey Resignation, which has seen nearly 400,000 older workers leave the workplace in the UK[35]. This will have consequences. In an ageing society, where we are all expected to work longer, it is a bare fact that companies are going to have to get better at incorporating and retaining their older colleagues.

There aren't many companies that are adopting 'age neutral' policies; the entrenched system of *age = stage at work* is still very much in place. But for how much longer? Gen X are not as rich as the Boomers, will not be able to retire as early, and will be required to stay active and keep learning and working well into the next decade.

What does looking after your older workers look like in the hybrid era? Eldercare policies, healthcare support for managing long-term illness, flexible career trajectories that enable people to downsize their career rather than retire and, crucially, a learning and development syllabus that caters for older workers. The age of the fifty-year-old apprentice is nigh!

5. The Knowledge Worker Revolution Is Feminised but Not Feminist

Let us first acknowledge how much the shift to flexible working has benefitted working mothers – the historic career losers in the remote working equation, who no longer have to endure those difficult conversations with their boss on whether to leave early for the nursery run or the school play. But something much more profound seems afoot. Last week, I gave a talk at an employee wellbeing conference and I was struck by how many stalls in the exhibition centre were advertising childcare offerings, fertility packages, and menopausal support for employees. They were addressing once silenced subjects and repackaging them as perks. This is testimony to the feminisation of the workplace, which has been decades in the making. But for it to be truly feminist, we must acknowledge that companies have a role to play in aiding men to step up in the domestic sphere. Key to this is implementing policies such as mandatory paternity leave (and probably eldercare leave) to relieve women of domestic burdens and countless hours of unpaid labour. That would be a truly feminist gesture, would be positively welcomed by millennial fathers who are already stepping up on the domestic front, and would also go a long way to reducing the gender pay gap. Some are paving a way, but we've a long way to go before such strategies become the norm. The workplace has encroached on the home; it's about time that the home encroached on the workplace.

7. Why Childcare Is a Business Issue
(Published: 8 September 2022)

Forget breakfast bars, gym membership, and even flexible working: if companies really want to get their millennial employees back into the office and earn their loyalty then why not support them with the burden of childcare? Sounds simple. Or is it?

The pandemic made us reappraise a lot of things in life, but ask any parent and they will probably say they have a renewed appreciation for childcare. As we parents were swamped under the impossible burden of having to entertain or home school our children while working, we came to realise just how fundamental childcare is, not just for our child's development or a mother's career prospects, but more specifically in enabling our dual-income households to actually function and stay sane. *We* recognised it, but did our employers?

For the last ten years the UK has had one of the most expensive and unworkable childcare systems in the world where, in some urban areas, we've come not to question the absurd practice, previously reserved for the very top private schools, of putting a baby's name down on a nursery waiting list even before the little bundle of joy arrives. And that is before parents are hit with the reality and cost. Despite the free childcare hours offered by government, two-thirds of parents pay as much each month towards their childcare as their rent or mortgage, according to a survey conducted by parenting website Mumsnet and campaign group Pregnant Then Screwed[36]. Single-parent families are particularly hard hit, as are those on universal credit where the childcare stipend is still calculated on 2005 costings[37]. This isn't news to parents, but may come as a shock to bosses who tend to think that their responsibility of paying wages each month is to keep a roof over their employees' heads, when for many the major outlay goes on the care infrastructure that frees up people's time to work.

This has long been the situation, but now childcare is at a critical juncture. According to recent data from the Institute for Fiscal Studies, the cost of a part-time nursery place for a child under two increased by sixty per cent in cash terms between 2010 and 2021 – twice as fast as average earnings[38]. Two-thirds of parents have seen an increase in childcare costs just this year[39] and this is likely to rise in the autumn as nurseries are confronted with inflated energy and food prices as well as staff shortages, and as existing local authority funding reduces in real terms. Nurseries have little option but to pass this burden on to parents, especially given that a third of UK nurseries are already operating at a loss[40]. Some are now charging £95 per day, or £1,900 per month, for one child to attend five days a week.

The problem is so acute that forty-three per cent of working mothers are considering leaving their jobs or working fewer hours due to childcare costs[41]. In the US, the situation is similar, if not worse. More than thirty per cent of families are considering taking a second job to manage the juggle[42]. As we know though, the pandemic forced many women to quit the workforce altogether. The number of women not in the labour market and looking after a family has risen by five per cent in the past year, the biggest leap in thirty years[43]. This is a consequence of the pandemic, which will have worrying ramifications for the economy as well as households. In the US, twenty-six per cent of women are out of work due to childcare costs and those women more likely to quit or reduce their hours are ethnic minorities and those on low wages; precisely those who should be supported[44].

I've spent the past two years helping companies navigate the post-pandemic work landscape and the most common thing I hear from CEOs and executives is that the Great Resignation, the war for talent, and the 'quiet quitting' of their Gen Z recruits constitute their major business concerns right now. But how many are considering the childcare crisis and its impact on their middle-aged millennial staff? They are the workers you've trained up and invested in. They are too expensive to lose.

Perhaps the reason for this oversight is the way in which society, government, and business holds on to a now outdated view that childcare is predominantly a women's issue; one that enables mothers to work. This is not how the majority of couples now see it or how they actually live. In an era where two-thirds of millennial couples are in two-wage families[45], when the cost-of-living crisis makes this a fixed necessity and where wage parity between couples has never been closer, it is recognised within the home at least that childcare is something that enables families to function, not just mothers to work. This again may feel alien to the CEO who perhaps has a stay-at-home wife or a full-time nanny.

But the time has come for business leaders to recognise that childcare, like other key areas such as health and pensions, is not the sole responsibility of employees but a fundamental business issue that impacts the bottom line and talent pipeline (as well as the gender pay gap). It shouldn't be framed as a 'nice to have' perk but rather, in the context of an economic crisis, critical support in ensuring that a key part of their workforce is able to actually turn up.

And for those who say childcare is a matter for government not businesses, it is worth harking back to the great entrepreneurial titans of the Victorian era for inspiration: those who built chapels, schools, housing, and entire towns not simply out of philanthropy and care but because they realised it made shrewd business sense. We could all look longingly at the favourable situation in Scandinavia – where in places like Denmark the average monthly payment is nine per cent of parental income – but that is not the reality across much of the developed world. Ireland, Australia, and Switzerland are just some of the countries where parents are spending above twenty per cent of their wages on childcare[46].

Thankfully, there are some companies that are leading the way. In the US, Californian progressive beacon Patagonia has established three childcare centres for its staff at a cost of more than a million pounds to the company. Positively, this has resulted in almost all working mothers returning to work after maternity leave and, most tellingly, it has had a profound impact on parents as a whole who are now twenty-five per cent less likely to leave than child-free employees. By Patagonia's own calculations, the savings in staff retention offsets thirty per cent of the actual outlay in running the nurseries[47]. Understandably, not all companies are willing to take on such a burden; a number are choosing instead to offer subsidised nursery places or reimbursements on childcare to parents. Bank of America, for example, provides a monthly stipend of up to $275[48] as well as immediate access to a doctor and prescriptions.

One of the major providers helping companies with these initiatives is Bright Horizons, whose corporate packages range from running on-site nurseries (such as that at Adobe) to childcare slots for employees or back-up childcare support in emergencies. They have just launched their personalised parental plan and over the course of 2020-21 established twenty-three employer-sponsored nurseries[49]. These, however, are isolated examples, as only eleven per cent of employers in the UK currently provide childcare packages as an employee benefit[50]. The advantages are obvious: it's an easy way of getting a millennial parent back into the office. It's also a decent short-term incentive for retention; you'd be less likely to change jobs if it also meant your child having to change nursery. It's also what employees want. In a 2021 survey of UK and US workers, Beamery found that care benefits were favoured over gym memberships, mental wellbeing support, and even paid parental leave[51].

In the time of the Great Resignation and the biggest squeeze on incomes since the fifties, making it easier for parents to work should not just be a business priority or a DEI initiative but an economic necessity. And governments should play a role too. Forget tinkering with corporation tax – why not offer tax breaks to companies who provide childcare i.e. help them help their employees? Support could also be given to the self-employed or company directors by enabling them to offset childcare costs against their tax bills. Why don't we recalibrate childcare, not as a family cost but as a business expense?

Company childcare schemes are a clear demonstration that you respect the care responsibilities and financial burdens of a key section of your workforce. Back in the fifties, companies made explicit efforts to satisfy the spouse to retain the husband. In 2022, it may be wise to start satisfying the child to retain the parents.

8. When Did Our Job Cease to Be Our Lifestyle?
(Published: 10 October 2022)

I recently had lunch with a man in his fifties who has spent most of his working life in the publishing industry. During our professional catch-up, it wasn't long before we hit upon the topic that most execs are talking about right now: dismay at Gen Z workers. The complaints were familiar: the lack of deference, unwillingness to work late, need for constant reward and handholding (his caricature, not mine). He then reverted to a natural reflex, something that afflicts anyone over thirty-five: comparing today's youth unfavourably with an airbrushed take on our younger selves. He harked back to his 'apprenticeship' years in the nineties: let's imagine lengthy lunches at the Groucho by day and champagne-filled book launches by night. Essentially, it was a tale where the commitment, hard work, and training were propelled (and made attractive) by lots of alcohol and lots of fun. 'That's the thing – these kids don't want to embrace the lifestyle that comes with the job'. But is he right?

Now I hate to generationally stereotype here but there is a definite type of Gen Xer – those in their fifties now, working in the creative arts broadly defined as journalism, TV, publishing, advertising, PR, fashion and so on – who will rhapsodise endlessly about the glory days of the nineties, back when pay was decent, business flights were the norm, and the entertainment allowance would make even a Dubai playboy blush. It was a unique moment when all those hapless humanities grads who had been told they'd only be fit for McJobs became masters of the universe. It was a time when working in the creative arts made you the barometer of aspiration, power, and cool. There is, of course, a similar narrative now happening in tech; it's not floppy-haired English grads these days but the Huel-sipping, jiu jitsu-wrestling computer geeks who have inherited the earth.

Anyway, it was around about 2008 when the wheels slowly started to come off the creative party bus. First came the financial crisis, when budgets were slashed, and then the digital revolution, which diminished everything these folks produced and ushered in today's era of algorithm-defined creativity. The sectors and workers did not vanish of course, but the status, money, fun, and the best bits of the lifestyle did. Millennials, who had grown up dreaming of glamorous jobs in TV, journalism, and advertising, and joined expecting to find such rewards, were soon disillusioned. Tech meant that they needed to work harder and play less. The more entrepreneurial ones tried their luck as digital creators, becoming its pioneers, while the creative sectors themselves lost their meritocratic kudos and became workplaces where only the affluent could afford to aspire.

Gen Z, who had grown up with their own publishing platforms and TV channels in their pockets, did not suffer from such illusions and are less disillusioned as a result. With the glamour, money, and lifestyle diminished in these sectors, what is left but a lifestyle that equals poor work-life balance? Gen Z's increasingly transactional approach to work (which is in fact a return to how we once thought about labour) is perhaps more understandable in these circumstances. All the while, the Gen Xer peeps in their fifties, at a career stage where they are personally buffeted from many of these challenges, sit at the top of the tree looking down, perplexed as to why those in their twenties don't lap up every opportunity as they once did.

In the knowledge economy, commitment and loyalty are often linked to short-term aspiration and the ability to see our future selves: 'Where and who will I be in five, ten years' time?' Many Gen Zers currently look at frustrated and struggling millennials and say, 'This is where your pursuit of purpose and late nights have got you; I'm unconvinced it's worth it.' Meanwhile, in the same vein, many millennials look up at Gen Xers at the top of the tree and lament the fact that their leaders are probably the last generation to enjoy such fruits.

It's not that the kids won't embrace the lifestyle; it's that they know the rules of engagement have changed. Each sector (and business) has its own story of course, but this point is in many ways universal, and yes, even in tech. So, however tempting it may be to compare Gen Z with our younger selves, it is not comparing like with like. We need to deal with and understand *how* they are, not just how we would want them to be.

9. Who Are Gen Z in the Workplace?
(Published: 22 November 2022)

'Don't take your laptop on holiday with you, you deserve a proper break,' my Gen Z employee instructed before I broke for half-term. Now, in contrast to when my husband makes such a suggestion, I'm prepared to listen to my new colleague on work/life balance matters for the simple reason that she appears to have achieved it. She has hobbies she invests serious time in, she knows when and how to log off, and she also knows how to work hard and prioritise what needs doing. In fact, over the past three months we've been working together, I've come to realise that I have a lot to learn from her about everything from office attire to liberation from email.

In truth, my education in the Gen Z work mindset began as soon as I advertised the post. The first thing I noticed was how quickly, and (often) without much thought, this generation are able to apply for jobs. The speed of LinkedIn meant that I had seventeen applicants within an hour of advertising (only one of them though had included a tailored cover letter, as requested). The LinkedIn algorithm means that job applications can be suggested to people even if they aren't even looking, which is a warning to employers – you're at constant risk of your best talent being poached. In that sense, the job market now mirrors the dating market more than ever and because of that, the interview process is now as much about the candidate getting the measure of the recruiter as it is the other way around.

Connected to this is Gen Zer's sense of worth. My new employee negotiated her salary with a resolve and a confidence that would never have occurred to me at her age. These kids know the value of money, having grown up under the shadow of 2008, and amid the ripples of Brexit and the panic of the pandemic. What with her side-hustle, she perfectly exemplifies a generation that knows its worth and the value of its time. This seems particularly game-changing for women, while it also points to the fact that Gen Zers will probably never fully subscribe to the one-salary mantra.

I've always worked a four-day week and tended to work from home, but it was my Gen Z who suggested regularised office days. She had worked fully remotely for the previous two years and recognised the negative impact it was having on her mental health and learning. And she was right. We are now in our new office two days a week and while it took me a while to adjust, I'm a complete convert. Working alongside each other, eating together, building social capital and friendship by discussing holidays and dogs, and yes, mutual learning, far outweighs anything I would have generated had she and I been fully remote.

And then there is the fashion: needless to say that I have never once seen her in heels. It's impossible not to notice the way that this generation of women dress in the post-#MeToo era. Gone are the tight LK Bennett dresses and commuter trainers (with heels in your bag), and in come the DM boots and baggy jumpers – fitting attire in an energy crisis but also an approach that rejects the old rules where women have so often been forced to put on a 'face', cultivate an image, and conform to someone else's definition of a professional environment. The pressure and price women have to pay for this is exhausting, which is why so many of us enjoyed hiding behind a camera in our sweatpants during lockdown. I admit I still blow-dry my hair on office days, but also feel less pressure to look a certain way.

I may have hit the jackpot with my Gen Zer, but the overwhelming reaction I've picked up from speaking to millennial and Gen X managers these past months about Gen Z is one of bemusement. Their concerns about Gen Z range from 'they don't respect us' to 'they can't answer the telephone'; from 'they just don't want to work as hard' to 'they have no interest in prioritising how this company makes money'. This last point was a common observation; Gen Z recruits don't seem to appreciate (or engage with) the core function of commercial reality and client growth.

In a sense these are justified complaints, but let's look at the context. On the phone issue, Gen Z grew up answering the phone in front of them rather than holding it to their ears – if they answered it all, that is, given the ubiquity of instant messaging. They never had the pleasure or the pain of having to phone a landline and speak to their friends' parents before they could speak to their friends. What feels like perfectly normal behaviour for the Gen Xer to pick up a phone to speedily resolve a work issue can be, for a Gen Zer, a deeply uncomfortable experience, unlike an email that allows composure time. Gen Zers are also massively underwhelmed by email as an efficient form of communication too. I've exchanged approximately four emails with my Gen Zer in as many months!

On the clients point, one aspect is clear: Gen Z want to personalise the work; they want to be closer to the cause or person that they are actually working for. If they cannot see the outcome of their input, they're never going to be fully engaged. I believe it will become increasingly important for Gen Z to be in the room and meeting the client (even if only to observe), so that they can connect their own contribution to the bigger project. The broader point concerns a culture of transparency that this generation is now demanding. They won't be satisfied tidying up a pitch deck and staying back at HQ while the grown-ups go and win the business. The satnav generation don't just want to be told the destination; they want to understand the journey.

'They don't respect us' was a common complaint from experienced managers. Well, no, they don't, at least not in the traditional sense, as they haven't been raised in a culture of deference, either in the home or at school; neither were millennials, by the way. Gen Z grew up in a culture where social media was the great leveller. They could publicly criticise a brand, politician, or service. Speaking truth to power comes naturally to them, which means, I'm afraid, that you are going to have to earn their respect rather than just expect it. And yes, that requires a lot more in person time.

Before you castigate Gen Z and their work habits, it is worth remembering that it is the aim of every generation to learn from their elders' mistakes. That is what being young is all about – challenging the status quo – and that is what Gen Z are doing on all fronts, whether it's rejecting the millennial staple of skinny jeans or expecting open conversations about work/life balance. Many of them grew up in dual-income households with both parents working. This was a major societal shift in the knowledge economy that also coincided with the digitalisation of the workforce, meaning neither Mum nor Dad could never truly switch off. What Gen Z is doing now is identifying the flaws, contradictions, or pressure points in the professional environment, and questioning it. The best thing we can do is to learn from their questions and, ultimately, start offering them some answers.

10. The Enduring Self-Sacrifice of the Office 'Team Mum'

You may not be familiar with the term 'Team Mum' in the workplace but I'm sure you will have encountered her. She's a staple in every almost business. She's the emotional bedrock, the one to whom everyone turns when they have problem, whether personal or professional. She's the fixer. She tends to exude certain qualities: approachable, informal, always 'on' and reliable, with an almost devotional approach to being everyone's problem solver – think Joan Harris in *Mad Men*.

I've spent the past two years talking to companies around the world on the future of flexible working and while the long-term impact of hybridity will take years to filter through, one thing is becoming clear: team mums are absolutely pivotal in making flexible working work for everyone's benefit – except their own.

I use the term 'Team Mum' because these individuals are disproportionately – but not exclusively – women. They also tend to be towards middling age and, invariably, in a management position. They do not necessarily have children but do take on a parental identity at work. And yes, I have met some 'Team Dads', but not many.

The success of flexible working was always going to rest in the hands of management rather than centralised leadership, but it is becoming clear that so much of the emotional and mentoring work is landing on the plates of the sacrificial few who are willing to take the time and expend the emotional energy required to absorb and solve other people's problems. As we encounter each other less in the office and are not afforded the time to forge new bonds or friendships with a suitable range of peers, mentors, and managers, it is no surprise that more and more of the burden is directed towards that one individual upon whom we can rely.

Nowhere is Team Mum's role more important than in parenting the new Gen Z recruits who entered the world of work during or in the aftermath of Covid, and whose needs their companies did not always suitably meet. Those recruits whose networks, learning, and socialisation have been curtailed and who, as a generation, are also much more predisposed than any other cohort before them to expect, and value, a more humane, personalised approach to management. These digital natives are, ironically, the generation that prizes face-to-face contact more than any other in the workplace, even though their own communication skills may be somewhat lacking. Although we must avoid lazy tropes about women being naturally emotionally intelligent managers, we can also presume that in an age when mental health is recognised, most of the informal help that is being offered to young people in our workplaces is being offered disproportionately by team mums.

I recognise this dynamic of parenting young people at work because this was once me. In my former life as a university lecturer, I slotted comfortably into my team mum identity, studiously learning the names of the 150 students under my supervision and spending additional hours holding their hands through the dissertation process. Word got round of my commitment and I found myself supervising students who weren't even signed up to my modules. Ultimately, this was to my detriment. These efforts weren't being recognised by the higher powers and what's more it was stopping me from finishing my book and focusing on my own goals. In the end, I left academia altogether.

And that is the real danger here for both companies and Team Mums themselves: something snaps. So what can be done? Team mums need to recognise the dangers of being a people pleaser and fixer at work and should be supported in setting boundaries. However, that's almost impossible if companies don't recognise the need to invest time and money in helping all staff, especially Gen Z, in generating their network and support base at work. And, even more crucially, firms need to create a culture in which team dads are as recognisable, approachable, and as effective as team mums. Informal support and management structures will always exist, but we can't simply rely on one or two parent figures to oil the wheels of office life. Team mums – and dads – need a break.

Chapter 2:
Generations As Consumers

1.   Who Are Gen Z Consumers?
(Published: 4 October 2018)

Zoe, seventeen, likes to switch off her phone and put it in another room so she's not distracted. Sitting on her bed, she opens her book and begins to read. 'I've really got into actual books – they are tangible, real, and my imagination can run wild,' she says with a genuine sense of wonder. She consumes anything from novels to non-fiction – especially works on feminism and art.

She used to purchase her items on Amazon but 'that took loooong, like twenty-four hours, to be delivered', so she's started going to her local library: 'It's great, the books are just there waiting for you.' Uploading a 'shelfie' of current reading material has become a popular status update among her friends.

Zoe's generation is rediscovering books in the same way that millennials discovered vinyl; the difference is that the former are increasingly doing it as a way of logging off from their smartphones. Last year, the psychologist Jean Twenge persuasively argued in *The Atlantic* that the device had destroyed a generation[52] – but was Twenge too hasty in that conclusion?

Zoe is a member of Generation Z (those born 1997-2010), who are very different from their millennial predecessors (those born 1981-1996). It is often remarked that whereas millennials came of age in the smartphone era, Generation Z are the social media generation. But the real distinction is that Gen Z are the ones who can't remember Myspace, think Facebook is for their parents, and see the Internet primarily as a video medium (using YouTube rather than Google to find something out).

If Facebook and Twitter turned millennials into commentators, then Snapchat and Instagram have turned Gen Z into broadcasters and storytellers. The average Gen Zers have had a smartphone since they were thirteen, which means they have had the misfortune of living most of their adolescence online.

Babyboomers are actually the fastest growing demographic on social media, revelling in the sensation of greater connectivity, but Gen Z – who have lived its realities and experienced its damaging impact on their time and mental health – are the ones questioning the point of it all. In the US, researchers at the University of Chicago found that fifty-eight per cent of teens said that they had voluntarily taken a break from social platforms in the last year[53].

In the same way that those who grew up with multiple TV channels now find the unlimited choice rather mundane, many teenagers feel they've reached iPhone saturation point. They speak of being 'phone-bored'; the feeling you get when you find yourself endlessly and aimlessly scrolling through your apps. Social media, as one sixteen-year-old boy put it to me, 'cannot make dull people interesting, plus there's only so many funny cat videos you can watch.' If such platforms thrive on keeping your attention, are they losing the attention of the young?

Some teenagers are logging off, others are embracing the novelty and freedom of 'dumb phones', such as the deliberately basic Nokia 3310, but it would be wrong to describe Gen Z as neo-Luddites. They are, however, developing a very sophisticated and obsessional interest in their data and privacy. Gen Z did not need the Cambridge Analytica revelations[54] to open their eyes to the fact that 'if the service is free, you are the product'. Unlike their elders, they have been aware of it since their tweens. They have been curating, collating, and uploading material for their online brand and filtering and 'spinning' their personal narratives for at least half of their lives.

Snapchat is their favoured app, precisely because the content disappears after ten seconds, although many find the Snap Map feature (locating the live whereabouts of their friends) a bit creepy. Many have both a private and a public Instagram account, and some have multiple profiles to reflect their many passions, fantasies and, increasingly, identities. Many opt not to use their real names or email addresses to access their platforms.

Gen Z is also using social media in more proactive, communitarian ways. While we can easily dismiss the virtue signalling 'clicktivism' of millennials (hashtags are the modern-day equivalent of pin badges), Gen Z, instinctively net citizens, are going above and beyond. Take, for example, the survivors and campaigners who emerged out of the Parkland shooting tragedy in the US. Though themselves too young to vote, their online campaign, which began as #neveragain, spiralled into a GoFundMe that raised four million dollars, a national school walkout, and companies from Delta to Hertz cutting ties with the NRA. It was remarkable in its speed, penetration, and tactics – not to mention far more effective in pressing for change in gun controls than years of conventional consciousness-raising.

Online campaigning for communitarian interests may be a minority sport, but commercial transactions for private gain are where Gen Z is really showing tech initiative. It is estimated that more than seventy per cent of today's teenagers are making their own pocket money[55]. And they are not doing a paper round or waitressing as in previous generations, but selling goods, clothes, or organising networks and events on social media. Depop, which has more than eight million users, offers their mostly young subscribers a cross between eBay and Instagram, enabling members to 'flip' second-hand clothes and trainers.

Many make a tidy profit and many more are learning a great deal about accountancy, photo editing, and marketing in the process. Scroll through the Depop marketplace and you will find teenagers exhibiting their items as if they were a fashion feature in *Vogue*. Depop now offers mentoring and support to would-be sellers, helping them to maximise their market's potential.

Companies have realised that the only way to reach this ad blocker generation – one that is unmoved by traditional, airbrushed, celebrity-endorsed advertising – is to sell their products via 'influencers' on social media. But more than this, companies are seeing the value of 'micro-influencers'; those with tens of thousands rather than hundreds of thousands of followers who are increasingly likely to get traction with a generation that prizes intimacy and authenticity.

This generation watches less than an hour of television a day, but four hours of YouTube. The popularity of vloggers lies not in their offer of escapism but their promise of an education (in whatever you are interested in, from how to code to how to apply eyeliner). YouTubers may be the new celebrity class to their millions of followers, but the truth is that all members of Generation Z consider themselves 'influencers'. That is the agency and perspective that the smartphone has given them.

But could it be that the touchscreen is destroying their sense of touch? A recent survey found that sixteen to eighteen-year-olds prefer 'sexting' to actual sex[56], with eighty-four per cent admitting to flirting and more than a third confessing they had sent a sexual or nude image via their phones.

It appears that this generation is on a continual loop of digital foreplay, preferring virtual to real interaction. They are also less likely to indulge in the traditional means of social lubrication that often underpin such trysts. In a survey carried out by the Office of National Statistics, less than half of UK eighteen to twenty-four-year-olds had consumed alcohol in the last week[57], compared with sixty-six per cent of the same age group in 2005.

'Sober socials' are now mainstream on university campuses and teenage pregnancy is now at its lowest rate for decades, but should we really be surprised, given that every bar a teenager walks into and every bed that they consider lying in now has a surveillance and recording device nearby? The potential for social shaming through video (not just photos) is so pervasive that it's no wonder that this generation are sensible and unrebellious.

The iPhone camera has achieved what years of sexual and drug education failed to do: prevented deviancy where public shaming is the ultimate deterrent. Teenagers live in fear of their misdemeanours being broadcast and will therefore do anything to maintain their brand. It is, however, this pressure to control other people's perception of them that is also leading to record levels of depression and anxiety.

Kids already groan about online 'sharenting'. An average child in the UK has more than 1,500 images of themselves shared on social media before they are five years old[58]. How long will it be before they start to use GDPR to remove the material?

'My mum needs to learn how to use social media properly,' said one fifteen-year-old girl I interviewed. 'She doesn't understand that what she posts about me I'm stuck with forever.'

There is a new slang word doing the rounds in the primary playground lately: *tapass*. It is what the kids call adults who are on their phones too much. If you think your child spends too much time on their phone, chances are they think the same about you.

Far from destroying a generation, the smartphone has conditioned them in sophisticated, surprising, and exciting ways the older ones are only really beginning to understand. And what they learn now will shape them in the future – whether as consumers, activists, voters, or entrepreneurs.

2. How Silver Surfers Are Taking over the Web
(Published: 22 April 2020)

In this pandemic era, any call or correspondence from my seventy-something mother is now treated (by her at least) as an urgent priority. Last week, within the space of two hours, she had sent me an email, quickly followed by a text message reminding me to read the email then a phone call to check whether I had. After all this nudging, I checked it, expecting something serious. It was a video of six ducklings being rescued from a drain on the US highway with the accompanying note: 'This is just lovely'.

My mother, who does not have a smartphone or social media accounts and still signs off her text messages 'Love Mum' (in case I'm unsure of the sender), had discovered the 'forward' button on Hotmail. My inbox is now clogged up with memes, video links, and weird emails asking me to forward the message to eight people to guarantee good fortune. This week we passed another major milestone: she joined Houseparty and made her first-ever video call.

Watching my mother's childlike wonder in discovering the glories of technology feels like watching myself experience the Internet back in 1999, except it isn't: in little over a week she has embraced a whole decade of tech innovation, from the forward button to video chat. And she is not alone. Paradoxically, while some millennials are using lockdown to enjoy a digital detox – indulging in what we may call 'boomer hobbies' of baking, gardening, or model making – their parents are switching on and discovering Web 2.0 in a big way, from video doctor appointments to internet banking and group Zoom calls.

In truth, silver surfers have been the fastest growing digital and e-commerce market for a while and are arguably as addicted to their smartphones as their children. A study in the US found that baby boomers were glued to their phones for five hours a day[59] (almost as much as millennials). According to Google, in the US they spend more time online than watching TV[60] and eighty-two per cent of boomers who use the Internet have a social media account (using an average of 4.6 different platforms)[61].

Facebook is the boomer's natural habitat to the extent that it is now called 'social media's retirement home'[62]. You may also say that it will soon become 'social media's graveyard', as according to the University of Oxford Internet Institute the number of dead profiles on Facebook will overtake the number of live profiles in a matter of decades[63].

As if in anticipation of this, the migration of boomers to Instagram is already happening, with the rise of the 'Instagran' and 'granfluencer' becoming a thing. Just check out @baddiewinkle, a ninety-one-year-old great-grandma from Kentucky whose profile is all millennial pink faux leather and feather boas and who has 3.8 million followers. Also @Irvinrandle, the sexy, hench granddad from Texas who has more than a quarter of a million followers and has taken to the catwalk.

Baby boomers are more predisposed to social media than any other generation; they are reportedly nineteen per cent more likely to click 'share' than younger cohorts[64]. This is harmless when it comes to not-so-funny memes, but worrying when it comes to nonsense about 5G and Covid-19, or any fake news for that matter. A study in the US found that people over sixty-five were more likely to be spreaders of fake news than all other adults[65]. Indeed, age was the most important variable, more significant than education, sex, or even political persuasion.

It's not that baby boomers are simply more gullible, but rather that they were taught to have an inherent trust in the old media and have simply transferred that trust to the new media. Younger cohorts, on the other hand, grew up with spam, clickbait, and deep-fakes and although their identities are more digitally entwined, they are also much more sceptical of what they see on screen. To understand this gap between the generations, it is also worth remembering that baby boomers grew up with just three television channels, whereas anyone under twenty grew up with their *own* channel.

It is easy to patronise baby boomers when it comes to their use of technology; so easy in fact that there is a Facebook page entirely devoted to it. A group 'where we all pretend to be boomers' has members echoing the traditional punctuation, earnest tone, overpraise, political prejudices, and conspiracy theories of baby boomers. It currently has more than a quarter of a million subscribers and might as well be called 'revenge of the snowflakes' who themselves have been stereotyped as lazy, entitled, and overly sensitive.

What is often at stake in the digital world, as in the real world, is not different values but simply different etiquette. My mother cannot understand why I never listen to her lengthy voicemails, though I still rely on her when it comes to the formalities of writing a proper letter ('Is it yours sincerely or yours faithfully?'). And before millennials start feeling smug, they too are old and are becoming an embarrassment. My sixteen-year-old cousin is appalled at how 'oldies' (meaning people in their thirties) are embracing TikTok in lockdown. Millennials may patronise their parents, but the kids are now holding their heads in their hands at us.

In these weird times, the 'techlash' has abated, and we all have a newfound gratitude for our ability to work, connect, and communicate virtually. My mother, lacking my weary scepticism, feels this keenly and quite rightly so; living alone in lockdown, technology has enabled her to see her grandchildren on their birthdays, have check-ups with her doctor, and feel part of the world outside her front door. Just please allow me to be grateful for the 'mute group' button on WhatsApp.

3. Why Boomer Widows Are the Only Influencers Who Matter
(Published: 16 May 2022)

Up until the point her husband died, Mary, seventy-two, had never paid a bill in her life. 'I was part of that generation who left all the financial decisions and admin to our husbands.' When Mary became a widow, it was a rude awakening. She discovered her husband had left unpaid debts, had loans from friends she never knew about, and a chaotic financial situation that took two years to sort out. She was at her lowest ebb but she emerged a different woman. 'I feel empowered like never before,' she said. It is little recognised, but widows such as Mary are fast becoming the most important powerbrokers in society. By 2025, sixty per cent of the nation's private wealth will be in female hands[66], with most of this inherited wealth from a deceased spouse.

We hear much about the 'Great Wealth Transfer' across the generations (estimated to be worth around £5.5 trillion over the next thirty years[67]) but there's a more immediate transfer happening right now: a great wealth transfer flowing between the genders. Two-thirds of baby boomer wealth is owned by joint households[68] and with many women outliving their husbands, they are set to be the major beneficiaries over the next decade – before their children get a look in. These women may have seen the flourishing of the feminist movement in their youth, and many worked before and after marriage, but when it came to major financial decisions and investing wealth, their husbands remained firmly in charge. So what happens when this cohort of women inherits their family wealth? I spent part of last year interviewing some of those women, trying to get a sense of what this great gender wealth transfer will mean for those widows, their families, and for the economy at large.

Women, as we know, have historically been the great caregivers in society, but arguably the boomer generation of women have performed those duties more profoundly than any other demographic before them. This has meant not only offering both financial assistance and a home to their millennial kids (who have had a stunted path into adulthood) but also quite often acting as chief caregiver for elderly parents – thirteen per cent of baby boomers spent lockdown looking after older relatives[69]. Let's also remember that the care responsibilities many women have can also extend to in-laws, distant relatives, and friends. I spoke to Lyn, seventy-five, who had inherited £350,000 from a friend whom she had nursed through a terminal illness. 'It doesn't feel like my money,' she confessed. Forecasters talk much about the inheritance economy, but in an age of longevity, increasing care needs, and parental dependency, this is overwhelming a female inheritance economy.

Women are more likely than men to pass on their money while they are still alive. This may mean that millennials have access to their inheritance sooner than they would have thought, but with the added pressure of Mum watching over their shoulders to see (and potentially having a say in) how they spend it. Little wonder then that we've seen so many millennials moving to be nearer Grandma and the rise of multi-generational households and holidays.

Forty per cent of grandmas in the UK provide regular childcare[70] and we are seeing millennial parents increasingly reliant on Grandma to co-fund their parenting; paying for nursery and school fees, tutoring, activities, and school trips. It could be that the real benefactors of the Great Wealth Transfer are not millennials at all, but younger generations: Gen Z and Generation Alpha. 'Be nice to Grandma' may well become the family mantra.

While many of the women I spoke to felt an obligation towards the immediate financial needs of their adult children, these women seemed far less concerned about their own long-term care needs. With women outnumbering men 3:1 in nursing homes[71], the social care crisis is overwhelmingly a female problem, so why aren't women planning for the inevitable? 'I feel too young to be thinking about it,' said Joy, 60. In the twenty-first century, when sixty is no longer considered elderly, Joy's words are a sign of society's progress but also point to denial around old age. Women make up fifty per cent of landlords in this country[72], indicating the historic tendency of women to put their money in what was considered a 'safe bet' – property rather than investments. Women are often categorised as risk averse when it comes to money and yet the bankruptcy rate amongst female baby boomers has increased by eighty-eight per cent over the last decade[73]; let's not assume that this inherited wealth is 'safer' in female hands. But one area into which these widows are likely to channel investment is in setting up their own businesses. Barclays has seen a dramatic 132 per cent increase of women over sixty-five opening business accounts, which represents the biggest leap of any demographic[74].

The phenomenon of the wealthy widow is unjust and uneven but also temporary. The cohort of younger women coming through is undoubtedly better educated, and many enjoy professional careers and years of financial independence before marriage, but they have nothing like the wealth of the boomers. Families too are changing, with rising rates of divorce, remarriage, and stepchildren complicating the inheritance economy even further. The women in their fifties that I spoke to had earned more of their own money but also seemed more preoccupied in spending it on themselves while they could still enjoy it rather than saving it for their children. This is played out in the statistics: in the US, women over fifty make up the largest demographic of incomes over $100,000, controlling ninety-five per cent of household purchasing decisions and eighty per cent of luxury travel purchases[75].

The *Sex and the City* Generation X women are not as rich as the baby boomers but are more likely to spend what they do have on themselves. Despite the obvious trauma and disruption of losing a spouse, widowhood is so often a moment of empowerment for women. For Mary it may have taken two years to sort out her finances after her husband died, but since then she has been determined to embrace new challenges: 'I went with four other women to Inner Mongolia to live in yurts with the locals, owls, and the camels – it was amazing!' said Mary, who is now planning on purchasing a house 'my husband would have hated'. Marketeers, financial advisers and advertisers trying to lure Gen Z on TikTok may be better off directing their energies towards Grandma on Facebook because that's where the real influencers can be found.

4.   Why Gen X Will Age Disgracefully
(Published: 27 May 2022)

Tattoos don't age well on maturing bodies. What starts as a bold statement on taut skin gradually fades and blurs into a saggy frame. After a midlife decade or two, those scripted Chinese wisdoms begin to look like a child has scribbled on your arm; those yin yang symbols resemble a smudged nightclub stamp on your inner wrist. Though ubiquitous now, it was Gen X (1966-1980) that popularised and personalised tattoos in the nineties. Today, we manipulate our bodies with an app; back then, the youth customised it with a needle. But in fading tattoos, do we have a clumsy metaphor for how Gen X will age?

Gen X has a unique place in history, sandwiched between baby boomers and millennials. They do not suffer from middle child syndrome; rather Gen Xers have always revelled in their mystery and exclusivity, like groupies of a band few have discovered. They've also revelled in being in the shadow of boomers (who tend to get the blame for younger generations' ills) although their intergenerational dynamic rests on the fact that Gen X comprises a much smaller cohort. Before writer Douglas Coupland gave them a label they didn't want, Gen X was known in purely demographic terms as the 'baby bust' (in contrast to the boom), reflective of the declining birth rate experienced from the mid-sixties. But in many ways, Gen X has always been associated with decline and, in turn, adaptation. Perhaps this is the source of their relative cynicism and DIY outlook.

Everything we associate with Western boomers is less true for Western Gen Xers in respect of their wealth, opportunity, and privilege. Likewise, everything we associate with millennials was in fact pioneered by Gen X, from work/life balance chat to food culture, from status travel to tech. They were the guinea pigs for personalised technology; the Sony Walkman kids who morphed into the Blackberry adults. They were the first generation to take a slower path into adulthood, with their McJobs and slacker mentality. They were the generation that saw a decline in marriage and women outnumbering men at university, setting in train a great disruption to the male breadwinner model. By the late 2020s, Gen X are set to finally overrun boomers[76] and their identity as a generation will morph once more, evolving (maybe reluctantly) into society's elders and, in doing so, redefine what it means to be old. But how will the kids of the seventies approach their actual seventies?

In a reversal of history over the last twenty years, we have come to associate retirement with wealth. That has been the boomers' experience, but it won't be the same for Gen Xers, who do not have anything like their predecessors' money. Gen X saw their savings and investments curtailed the most of any generation during the financial crisis and even though they recovered, it is still striking that in the US Xers hold 28.7 per cent of the wealth compared with the 51.8 per cent belonging to boomers[77]. Gen X has more debt than any other generation[78] (partly because they are in their peak debt years), but many in the US are in the tricky situation of still paying off their student loans while also financing their children's education.

Gen X's financial precarity will have knock-on effects for the family. It is unlikely that they will be able to support their Gen Z kids in the same way that affluent boomers have carried their millennial children. Today, the 'Bank of Mum and Dad' typically lends £6bn a year, making it the equivalent of a top-ten UK mortgage lender[79], but that probably won't be the case in twenty years' time. As a consequence, Gen Z may be less preoccupied with homeownership, more self-reliant, and even more politically frustrated than millennials. Gen X, though, may find that many of their retirement years and funds are taken up with caring for their elderly parents. This will be particularly true for Gen X women (the main carers, even of their in-laws), but it will conflict with the fact that this female demographic is more financially independent than its predecessors, has worked more, and will want to work longer.

Gen X was also the first cohort to experience significant growth in remarriage and 'blended families', which will no doubt complicate inheritance and care responsibilities in later years. Similarly, Gen X has seen the rise of those with no dependents at all which, although liberating in midlife, poses particular difficulties in old age. Will Gen X be the one to pioneer 'chosen family' models of care as a result?

More than any other generation before them, Gen X women tended to marry men closer in age and of a similar economic and educational status. Add to that the fact that the life expectancy gap between men and women is narrowing, and there's the potential that the historic life-stage unique to women – widowhood – may be cut short or even go into decline. Currently, women outnumber men 3:1 in nursing homes[80], but for how much longer? The gender gap will close just as the social inequality gap widens among the elderly. Gen X will also be the most diverse elderly generation in history: goodbye to the unwritten assumption that an old person equals white and affluent. Just as we are rightly seeing a revolution in representation happening in younger generations, so a similar shift will be triggered in how we see and reflect old people in society, not just in adverts but across politics, policies, and planning.

But it is in the world of work that Gen X will really reject the status quo. The UK state pension age is sixty-six, but Gen X already knows this is irrelevant. And while many will continue to work out of desire, many more will do so out of need. Gen X entered the job market as final-salary pensions were being withdrawn but before auto-enrolment got going. Forty-one per cent of Gen X Americans[81] and thirty-three per cent of Brits fear they do not have enough in their savings[82] to see them through old age, while sixty per cent of Americans[83] and sixty-two per cent of British Gen Xers[84] see themselves seeking additional income in retirement, chiefly through part-time work. Gen Z parents won't be able to rely on Grandma for childcare like their millennial predecessors: she will probably still be working.

The problem though is that few companies are built for retaining an older workforce. Young people are cheap; experience is expensive. Redundancy rates for those aged between sixty and sixty-four are twice as high as those for people aged between sixteen and forty-nine. Add in the complication of age discrimination, lack of training for older employees, and automation and it is hard to see how Gen

X's desire to work for longer will be easily accommodated. Companies will need to adapt, probably by offering lower-status, lower-paid, part-time work for older employees. Will retirees consider downsizing their careers in the same way as they currently downsize their homes?

Inevitably, there will be a natural flow into the gig economy. Now a well-established route pioneered by the boomers, the rise of the 'grey gig economy' is reflected in the fact that fifty per cent of the UK's self-employed are over fifty years old[85]; a figure that can only increase. But, as we know, in the gig economy there are winners and losers; what is freedom for some is, for others, a debilitating lack of security. We currently assume the delivery economy is a young man's game, but we may soon find our pizzas and parcels being dropped off by an elderly person seeking to bolster their state pension.

The major obstacle to these plans, though, is their health. Gen X are in worse physical shape than baby boomers were at their age[86] and while life expectancy has been on an upward trajectory, this has translated into more years of ill-health rather than those in good health. Gen X are the first generation to have decades-long exposure to the ills of modern life: a sedentary lifestyle, processed food, earphones, blue light, and a fitness culture that at the very least means bad backs and arthritic knees and at worst means diabetes and obesity. Strikingly, seventy-eight per cent of Gen X men are overweight in the UK[87]. Given that fact, it seems logical that Gen X will be the ones most willing to invest in preventative and monitory digital healthcare. The latchkey kids of the seventies started life with keys around their necks and will end their lives wearing pendant alerts.

Gen X are currently navigating the social care crisis for their parents, and this is inevitably impacting their own attitudes towards their end-of-life care. Put simply, Gen X will have higher expectations, from LGBTQ-only residencies to complexes for the affluent that feel like a Soho House hotel. The playlist will need to change, too, of course: think mobility classes to 'Firestarter' rather than the 'Hokey Cokey' and sing-alongs to Lauren Hill rather than

Vera Lynn. This tech generation will also be more open to innovative forms of automated care: in-house robots may make sense to a generation that grew up with Tamagotchis. Likewise, we may see more of the elderly remain in cities. There's already a move by major care providers to build residencies in metropolitan areas, giving older people greater independence and more connectivity. As flexible working allows younger generations to flee to suburbia and the countryside, older people are moving back into the city. We tend to assume great metropolitan hubs are places of street fashion, cutting-edge tech, and youthful vibrancy, yet the metropolitan future could be very different, or certainly more multi-generational.

But what does all this mean for politics? For a long time, politicians have played to the boomers' tune, protecting asset prices and the green belt (that was where the votes were, after all). Gen X will not carry the same political weight or power. But in an ageing society, where by 2030 half of all adults will be over fifty, politics will remain weighted towards the elderly and will be reflective of their evolving needs. That will mean promises to protect the rights of the old at work (from redundancy and retraining) alongside pledges on social care and equalising the inheritance economy.

As a society we tend to focus on evolving youth culture and to equate that with the future. We are less predisposed to reflect on how those at the opposite end of the lifecycle are evolving, in arguably more profound and innovative ways. It may be then that the future of driverless cars will be most readily adopted by Gen Xers, who currently represent the biggest percentage of car buyers[88]. Perhaps the chief traders in NFTs will be Gen X who, as the original 'musos', will invest their savings in tokens of their favourite band's back catalogue. And perhaps Gen X will be the powerhouse behind the metaverse, buying up memorial sites to preserve a digital afterlife. Who could have predicted baby boomers dominating Facebook and achieving super-host status with their second homes on Airbnb?

One thing is certain: Gen X will represent the last of the decadents – the generation who still found joy in alcohol and in the romanticism of taking drugs and being out of control before the great social media purge. Perhaps that will be their identity as society's elders. Gen X will reminisce about the olden, golden days of the nineties like the boomers talk about the sixties as a dose of hedonism in contrast to today's puritanism. The fading tattoo, then, is a terrible metaphor for how Gen X will transition into the last phase of their lives. Instead of fading out gradually, they will live longer, work longer, and expect more.

5.   The Dangers of Quick Credit for Gen Z
(*UnHerd*, 10 June 2020)

If you want to find out what Generation Z is thinking, look at what's trending on TikTok. One meme, seen millions of times during lockdown, has been the #GoHard video, featuring a comedic lip-syncing sketch to the US rapper Kreayshawn's lyrics: 'I'd really like to do that but I don't have any f***ing money'. The meme reflects the frustrations of wanting to do something and then discovering a genius way to do it without needing to pay. Several feature 'buy now, pay later' payment app Klarna as the 'solution'.

Any company would bend over backwards for such authentic, fun — and free — advertising; it reflects the Swedish finance firm Klarna's growing Gen Z-centred customer base. Klarna has been operating in the UK since 2017 and has now linked up with more than 4,500 major retailers, from H&M to JD Sports. This and other, similar, apps such as PayPal Credit, Clearpay, and Laybuy enable online customers to either delay or divide the payment across multiple weeks — without incurring interest.

These apps have been godsends for online shoppers during the pandemic because of the way they enable the consumer to purchase several items, try them then send unwanted ones back before they have officially paid for them, meaning that shoppers are not caught up in the inconvenience of delayed reimbursement from retailers. It enables consumers to literally 'try before they buy' even when the shops are all shut.

One TikTok meme sees parcel after parcel pile up on a bed with the tag: 'Klarna getting me through lockdown one ASOS package at a time'. This trend is real: the price comparison site comparethemarket.com found that twenty-three per cent of Gen Z have turned to 'buy now, pay later' services during lockdown[89]. While many of us are feeling rather smug about all the savings we are making during this enforced period of restrictive spending[90], some are experiencing the opposite: online spending sprees funded through delayed payment apps mean that they risk emerging out of lockdown with significant amounts of debt.

'Keep thinking I'm saving money in lockdown and then I remember my FAT Klarna bill,' tweets one customer. For a large proportion of this generation, whose status emanates from an ever-evolving visual identity through social media, lockdown has been a case of 'you can't change your location but you can change your clothes'. With Klarna operating as the default payment option at the checkout on some sites, it's easy to see why it is so alluring: as a convenient, flexible alternative to store and credit cards it appears to be a wholly benign form of debt.

Problems can arise, however, if you miss a payment that, with bi-weekly instead of the usual monthly payments, is all too easy to do. Klarna itself has estimated that consumers spend on average fifty-five per cent more when they are given the option of delaying or paying over several weeks[91] (without admitting that this may be money customers do not have). Email and text reminders are sent, but the account will be sent to a debt collection agency when customers fail to act. Klarna has said that it has clear T&Cs, a strict vetting process, and responsive customer services, but an investigation by *The Daily Telegraph*[92] found that 30,000 customers have already had their credit damaged because of missed payments.

As debt services go, it would be wrong to put Klarna in the same class as Wonga or Brighthouse (which, incidentally, folded during lockdown) but we are right to question their corporate responsibility when this service is so quick, easy, and marketed chiefly at the young. With its millennial pink logo and its focus on social media influencers such as *Love Island* contestants, Klarna has successfully tapped into a tricky market that can often elude major retailers. Its recent campaign 'Shop like a Queen' was a deliberate appeal to the LGBTQI community, sponsoring the former *Ru Paul's US Drag Race* stars Katya Zamolodchikova and Trixie Mattel's YouTube show *UNHhhh*.

But a generation that has had smartphones in their palms since their early teens is wary of crude endorsements. One US viewer complained on Reddit that he was 'disappointed' to see *UNHhhh* 'turn into an extended commercial for [a] credit scheme'. This generation, which grew up in the wake of the 2008 financial crash, also takes a sceptical view of investments, the stock market, and established moneylenders. According to the consultancy firm Cassandra, only thirty-four per cent of Gen Z trust banks[93].

Gen Zers are wired differently to millennials when it comes to consumption, debt, and saving. Whereas millennials grew up in the boom years, a Gen Z childhood (when your attitudes towards money are formulated) was defined by the 2008 financial crash, followed by austerity and sluggish recovery in the wake of the Brexit referendum. They watched their parents struggle and will themselves experience the post-Covid crash. They won't able to rely on the Bank of Mum and Dad in the same way that a significant number of millennials did.

They also grew up during the fintech revolution, during which automated payments and cashless transactions became the new normal, and the weight of coins in your pocket became an alien sensation. Add to that the era of fast fashion and fast consumption and you have a generation that is on the one hand much more prudent than millennials in valuing money, but also much more vulnerable when it comes to spending it.

The combination of tech and tough times has made them more resourceful and more entrepreneurial — a number generate their own money from a younger age. They are also savvy shoppers, to whom price comparison is second nature, while their ethical credentials and fashion-conscious aesthetic have triggered a revolution in the second-hand clothes market that rivals that of fast fashion. **Depop**, a buying and selling app, has experienced a ninety per cent increase in traffic since 1 April.

There are signs that they are more inclined to save than millennials too. When HSBC ran a survey asking Gen Z and millennials what they would do with £1,000 cash, seventy-two per cent of Gen Z (compared with fifty-five per cent of millennials) said they would put it into a savings account[94]. The challenger bank Monzo, an app-only bank whose card is now a staple in every Gen Z wallet, catered for the new banking priorities of young people post-crash who wanted greater control over their finances through its spending notifications and saving pot features. It also recently signed a deal with the saving app Emma[95], which it plans to launch for those as young as eleven.

Generation Z may see the benefits of saving, but they also have a more relaxed attitude towards spending and debt. Student loans have normalised debt for the young but not given them the skills to manage it. Debt, of any kind, has been made to feel inconsequential. As one commented on TikTok when responding to a #GoHard Klarna video: 'I have a debt collection agency after me for a £15 ASOS order' — complete with a laughing emoji. The social shame of living on the never-never, common up until the eighties, is not something that bothers this generation.

Nor perhaps does the prospect of insolvency. Bankruptcy claims among the young have increased tenfold in three years: under-25s now account for 6.5 per cent of all cases, according to the accountancy firm RSM[96]. One debt advice company estimated that this demographic represented fourteen per cent of all clients in 2018, with an average debt of £6,000[97]. A study found that eighteen per cent of eighteen to twenty-four-year-olds use their credit card for bills and essentials[98].

The success of these apps also lies in the fact that Generation Z, more than any other generation, has been conditioned to the 'one-click' transaction. Apps such as Klarna do not just encourage the 'I want it now' urge but also normalise the frictionless buying experience. This was pioneered by Amazon and Apple but, in the case of Klarna, is financed through debt.

The move to a cashless society has meant that all ages have experienced a growing detachment and responsibility from the transaction — the psychological difference between a couple of clicks online and physically handing over cash. This becomes problematic when it is a debt-based transaction involving someone young and financially vulnerable who is used to one-click credit and has an easy attitude towards debt. Parents have been talking to their kids about the perilous nature of social interactions online; it could be that they also need to start educating them on the perilous nature of financial transactions online too.

But beware lecturing the young on money. The days of delayed gratification are long gone for most of us. Generation Z are no more consumerist than their parents, and certainly more financially inventive, informed, and resourceful than millennials. Some responsibility must lie with companies themselves in providing full transparency of terms, thorough checks on vulnerable customers, and a genuine commitment to responsible debt control. The debt industry will always work out new methods to lure consumers. For the majority debt is a convenient and, if managed, perfectly sound financial behaviour. But we are facing a fierce financial headwind that has already disproportionately impacted the young.

One bruised Klarna customer on Reddit offered a solution: 'Saving seems to be an act of resistance.' To Gen Z – a savvy, activist generation – recalibrating shrewd financial behaviour into a political act might just gain traction.

6. How Millennials Are Becoming Old and Domesticated
(*UnHerd*, 16 June 2020)

Livestock farmers know more than most how to contain the spread of disease. As Roni Lovegrove, a cattle owner from Kent, explained to me, 'Once you get to a certain density level, pathogens run riot. High density means disease. Lower density is the only way to ensure you don't wipe out your stock. It's a constant juggle, calculation, and effort.'

This public health lesson is one that the Victorians knew all too well and yet we are having to learn it again nearly two centuries later as businesses restart post-lockdown. Let us not underestimate how difficult this will be, not because of stifling government regulation (one metre or two?), nor because of consumer fear, but because our very economic model is based on high density.

The Tesco founder and First World War veteran Jack Cohen, who used his de-mob money to set up a market stall in London's East End, had one abiding business principle: 'Pile it high, sell it cheap'. The approach became the chief characteristic of twentieth-century consumption in every sector from groceries to restaurants and from beauty to air travel.

Once the epitome of luxury and exclusivity, air travel had opened up to the masses by the nineties. The new model was all about low costs and high volumes. That marvel of engineering and design, Concorde, was grounded just as upstart low-cost airlines such as Ryanair built their brand by stripping back add-ons and offering absurdly cheap seat sales. Middle-market companies such as British Airways had no choice but to follow suit and lower their prices. The 'no frills' competition reached the grocery sector too, with Lidl, Iceland, and Aldi chipping away at market share. Their success lay in winning over middle-class consumers for whom 'bargain bragging' about a £10 flight to Florence or grocery savings became *de rigueur* at dinner parties.

Whereas the consumer boom in goods relied on an increasingly globalised and cheap supply chain, the consumer boom in experiences — be it travel, eating out or a haircut — centred on tight margins and low prices funded by boosting capacity. If density is its founding principle, then social distancing puts that entire model in jeopardy as consumers begin to prioritise space and safety above cost, and businesses recognise they can only survive by raising prices to counter lower footfall.

Restaurant owners, who all work on an extremely fragile business model, are especially vulnerable. In a survey by Square Meal, three-quarters of bar and restaurant owners said they did not think their establishment would survive social distancing[99]. What of those restaurants with long benches designed like a school canteen where you are so close to fellow diners you end up eavesdropping on their conversations? And will a bar that is only running on sixty per cent capacity have the same ambience? For every punter happy to get a seat, there will be others who miss the buzz of a busy bar.

Jo Eames, director of Peach Pubs, stated that 'margins are so tight and costs so high in hospitality that no business can operate for long with much less than ninety per cent full turnover'[100]. Social distancing reduces capacity and will result in job losses and higher prices. Those restaurants in the City or the West End, with high rents dependent on international tourists and business lunches, may end up faring much worse than small local establishments who are able to diversify their service with home deliveries, cooked-to-order meals and an add-on specialist grocery store.

Hair salons are another case in point. Hairdressing is modelled on the Ford assembly line with stylists, colourists, and apprentices allotted designated roles and slots. Under this system, one stylist has the capacity to work on three clients over three hours. This becomes impossible under the new rules; stylists may have to stay with one client for the duration, massively impacting the numbers that will be able to come through the salon door, which will inevitably push up prices. But the salon experience too will be diminished with the removal of the waiting area, refreshments, magazines, and the installation of inhospitable Perspex shields between chairs.

The high-density model made everything more accessible and also fed a culture in which consumers prioritised the buying of experiences over the buying of things. This was especially true for the millennial generation, which was priced out of the housing market. What became cheap as they came of age — technology, eating out and travel — were all things, unsurprisingly, that millennials loved spending their money on. More millennials have passports than driving licences, which is testimony to the fact that the open sky rather than the open road has long been the symbol of millennial consumer identity (compared to their gas-guzzling baby boomer parents).

For millennials, 'keeping up with Joneses' was not about your car, home, or stuff owned; we could rent, share or borrow that stuff anyway. No, our status derived from something different: our experiences — the places we went, the people we met, the things we saw — and crucially the documenting of those experiences on social media. It is not the selfie that defined us, but the representation of the self captured in the moment at a concert, in a restaurant, on a beach.

But now the crowd has been dispersed and the experiences have been put on ice. In a post-Covid world, it's the home that represents a safe haven while everything that millennials enjoy spending their money on has been curbed. Evidence for this lies in how much money this particular demographic has saved over the past three months. According to Barclays, the savings balances of eighteen to twenty-nine-year olds have increased by 9.9 per cent, with an average saving amount of £604; eleven per cent more than the national average and the highest of any age group[101]. According to Ipsos Mori, while shopping habits did not really alter for those aged between fifty-five and seventy-five under lockdown, they changed the most for millennials, who bought different products and in different quantities than they did before[102].

But as lockdown is eased, will millennials (in particular) resume their normal ways? Will we see an era of 'revenge spending', (a term first coined in China, which saw an initial uptake in designer items being purchased after lockdown eased)? Consumer analysts and the Government hope that 'pent-up demand' will result in a spending splurge — and the long queues outside Primark yesterday certainly point to that. The Barclays consumer survey however reveals that for millennials, the immediate priorities are restaurant meals and getting a haircut. It also revealed that thirty-seven per cent of millennials would like to be more attentive and responsible with their finances[103].

But good intentions often wane. What may be more significant is that millennials could be forced into different spending habits due to changing prices. It has been estimated that package holidays could rise by £1,000 per head[104] (not accounting for rising insurance costs). In the short term, there may be lower fares to entice customers back, but with airline bankruptcies and reduced competition, an inevitable decline in business travel, and consumer fear likely to be a lingering factor, airlines will need to make even more money from their economy-class consumers. As one travel agent put it to me: 'The days of flying so far, so often and so cheaply are over' — a fact that will chime with millennial and Gen Z's environmental concerns.

As if pre-empting this shift, Airbnb has already sacked twenty-five per cent of its workforce[105]. It may be that, paradoxically, millennials end up benefiting. If over-tourism becomes a thing of the past and all those empty commercial office properties are turned into flats, the urban housing and rental market may finally become more affordable.

Airbnb is already refocusing its attention away from rental business to what they call 'Air Experiences'; recalibrating the experience economy for the digital realm (clumsily known as 'phygital'). Pitched as 'unique activities we can do together led by a world of hosts', you can take your pick from an art tour of Lisbon, a water blessing meditation ritual with a Bali-based Monk or a virtual trip through Chernobyl with its abandoned dogs — all within the comfort of your home.

For people in their thirties who were already feeling an acute sense of burnout, with a family or soon to start one, and desiring greater flexibility at work, lockdown only reinforced what they already knew. A tiny pod apartment or flat share in the centre of town, especially surrounded by closed shops and lifeless bars, has its limitations. So even if we do snap back into old routines in twelve months' time, things will be different in the long term, in part because business models will have had to change to survive but also because new habits and values will have been formed. As long as the economic incentives are there, a significant number of them will be encouraged (and possibly forced) to make the same choices as their parents, shifting from being buyers of experiences to buyers of stuff and assets.

It will mean the birth of the 'homebody economy', where millennials invest in their houses as a home beyond a crash pad. Lockdown saw one-quarter of millennials increase their purchase of home, garden, and DIY products. A move triggered by lockdown will be sustained because of new priorities — not least the inevitable and hugely significant shift in flexible working.

Might we see the rise of a new demographic — the suburban or semi-rural millennial — in their detached houses with their detached phygital dinner parties? Can we envisage a twenty-first-century millennial mashup of Mike Leigh's seventies satirical play *Abigail's Party*, where couples share a simultaneous delivery from their favourite restaurant, give virtual tours of their renovated home office, bark orders at their Alexas and share Spotify dinner party playlists while wistfully reminiscing about the good old days of music festivals and cheap adventure travel?

Now that really would be a status update.

7. Why Each Generation Thinks It Knows What Good Parenting Looks Like
(June, 2022)

Admit it, we've all done it: made snap judgements of others' parenting. But it takes a brave soul to vocalise it.

I have been called both a bad mother and a good mother by random members of the public. On one occasion, on a hot, packed Tube – the day of an England World Cup match no less – I and my then two-year-old son were engaged in quite a rough tussle with a Slinky. I was interrupted by a man who informed me that I was overstimulating my child and that it would be best if I left my son alone. My reaction was naturally incandescent rage. The man may have been right, but he didn't know the context: my father had just passed away, it was one week from my wedding, and I hadn't seen my son all day.

On another occasion, I was in a cafe playing 'guess which hand it's in' with the only suitable item in my handbag, a tampon, in order to distract my very hungry daughter while we waited for our order. A lady passed by and informed me how nice it was to see a mother entertaining her child with something other than a screen. Again, she was unaware of the context: my daughter had spent the morning in front of *Cocomelon* while I worked. It is worth pointing out that in both incidents this feedback on my parenting came from older people – probably parents, possibly now grandparents.

But far more often, such awkward exchanges are happening within families rather than between strangers. In a recent US poll, forty-three per cent of parents said they had been in conflict with grandparents over the parenting of their children. And many of those conflicts remain unresolved, with fifty-three per cent of grandparents refusing to change their approach even after a plea had been made.

In the UK, grandparents save families thousands per year by providing informal childcare and, with the rise of multi-generational living and millennial financial dependency on the Bank of Mum and Dad (a lot of which is spent directly on the grandchildren), the stage is set for an intergenerational collision in parenting priorities and styles. Nowhere is this clash more pronounced than in first and second-generation immigrant families where the economic power play may be less obvious, but the expectation of adhering to tradition is more intense.

So, what are the areas of dispute? It depends on which generation you speak to. According to one US survey, grandparents bemoaned the lack of parental discipline as well as displaying differing priorities on manners, respect and money. Grandparents overwhelmingly believed that parents gave their children too much power. According to parents though, forty per cent said that disagreements occurred because grandparents were too lenient on the child. They can't even agree on what they disagree on. Not all families, of course, experience such tensions, and I'm sure there are many who live in a harmonious, multi-generational bubble. For many though, the tussle can feel undermining and unresolvable on both sides. And quite often, it is the major source of intergenerational, predominantly female, tension within the family. But why is that so?

The reason is part personal, part social. Becoming a parent required, for me at least, the forging of a new identity and, given I was well into my thirties when I had my first child, it took me a couple of years to find my confidence and style. It certainly didn't happen the moment I got pregnant, or gave birth; it was probably only when I was faced with a recalcitrant toddler with his own voice and teeth. It is a fact rarely acknowledged that in this era of multi-faceted and fluid identities, motherhood too requires a transition, possibly constant transition, as your children grow. And because it is so intimately personal but so often on public display, it comes with an inevitable degree of defensiveness and quite often results in an unspoken yet real divide within the sisterhood. Put bluntly, any criticism or observation, however small, cuts deep.

And, as much as parenting is about nurturing the next generation, it also naturally prompts a reconciling with one's own childhood.

Every parent seeks to learn from (even if they are doomed to repeat them) the mistakes of their parents. And this desire is particularly felt by the millennial generation who, for good or ill, have been nurtured in a culture of self-analysis and self-improvement. Yes, it may be optimistic, but millennials feel compelled to break negative intergenerational cycles more than any other generation before them.

The reason also lies in the new social context in which we are now operating. The twenty-first century parenting landscape of gender reveal parties, hypnobirthing, and 'sharenting' on social media is understandably incongruous to older generations. But then today's parents reflect in disbelief that doctors were once accepting of smoking during pregnancy and that parents used to put babies to sleep on their stomachs and were encouraged to train away left-handedness in their children. Is there an area that is more subject to changing advice and evolving trends than parenting?

Millennial parents are navigating challenges that their boomer counterparts did not have to contend with; principally twenty-four-hour hand-held interconnected tech. It's a burden they feel keenly: in a poll conducted before the pandemic, two-thirds of US parents said that parenting is harder today than it was twenty years ago, a fact the majority put down to technology. But consider that the next generation of parents may have to deal with something even more challenging: a world lived entirely through an all-encompassing virtual headset. The point is that there are broader and evolving forces at play; tech, economics, the built environment, working culture, changing gender relations, not to mention global pandemics, that are equally as pivotal as the personal in determining the kind of parent you and your peers become.

So if millennial parents find themselves preaching on the amount of sugar in baked beans to the generation for whom it was a household staple, or on the dangers of microplastics to the generation whose toys were laced with lead paint, or calling out racist, body-shaming, or gendered language to a cohort raised on Benny Hill, then this is in part because parenting is the moment when societal shifts become ingrained in the individual; when one generation finally breaks out to align with the next. Each generation of parents feels compelled, quite rightly, to not only learn from past mistakes but to also prepare the child for the world as it is, not as it was. In other words, the generation gap in parenting is real and also the natural order of things.

And in a society where families are smaller and women are having babies later (and therefore find themselves completely divorced from the world of birthing, breastfeeding, education, and being young by the time they have children), it is little wonder that parents have increasingly turned to experts for help. Between 1975 and the nineties, the number of parenting books increased five-fold. For the millennial generation, it's now become a maxim that Google has replaced Grandma. Each cohort of parents seeks out gurus to show them another way and to help them figure out their generational parental identity.

It was in fact the boomers who, as babies, were the first generation exposed to parenting experts. In 1946, Dr Spock's *Common-Sense Book of Baby and Child Care* set the scene for a new style of post-war parenting that rejected the previous belief that children should be seen and not heard and instead prioritised the emotional wellbeing of the individualised child. Out went outdated notions that breastfeeding was animalistic and that babies shouldn't be fed on demand. Dr Spock's advice, leaning heavily on Freudian analysis, was to trust your instincts, shower children with affection, and treat them as individuals. His book would go on to become the third best-selling book of the twentieth century, after Shakespeare and the Bible. Twenty-six pages of advertising accompanied Dr Spock's seminal text, proving there's nothing new in the commercial exploitation of anxious parents.

When boomers became parents, it precipitated a new wave of advice. Heidi Murkoff kicked off in 1984 with *What to Expect When You Are Expecting*, setting in motion a culture of maternal bodily self-regulation and responsibility: out went smoking and in came listening to Mozart to improve the babies' brain function. Boomers were encouraged to be more invested and individualistic in their parenting, with educational attainment the ultimate aspiration. The nineties gave birth to the helicopter mum, always hovering near, monitoring progress and safety in a structured environment. Running parallel was a new fashion for maternal naturalism pioneered by Dr William Sears, whose attachment parenting theory advocated co-sleeping and breast-feeding into toddlerhood. Amid it all, were we getting any closer to raising the perfect generation of kids? No: those experts were merely reflecting the new needs and anxieties of their chief audience, and a growing one at that – the degree-educated working mother.

And today, as millennial parents take the helm, a new consensus and fresh expectations are being forged: parents who see the current mental health crisis in teens and are committed to building emotional resilience in their toddlers; parents who themselves bear the scars from the 'sink or swim' education system and are instead encouraging creativity, play and an acceptance of failure; parents who fear the dependency on screens and fixate on forest school as the antidote. Helicopter parenting is out of fashion, only to be replaced with 'pilot parenting': the idea that parents share in the experience alongside the child, whether it be craft making or watching TV. Today, working mothers spend just as much time with their kids as stay-at-home mothers did in the seventies. This new expectation on 'quality time' is social tyranny – costly in terms of time and money, socially exclusionary, and increasingly impossible in dual-working households during a cost-of-living crisis.

One certainty is that yet another reckoning will come, probably when Generation Alpha enters the workplace and their Gen Z managers are confronted with a workforce they can neither understand nor manage (just as they become parents themselves). It all points to an overarching truth: if company bosses really want to understand how to manage the generations, they would do well to look at the history of parenting – the evolving trends wherein each generation is forged and where the generation gap truly begins. And for those parents and grandparents clashing over parenting styles, I recommend that both seek comfort in the words of Philip Larkin:

This Be The Verse

They fuck you up, your mum and dad.
They may not mean to, but they do.
They fill you with the faults they had
And add some extra, just for you.

But they were fucked up in their turn
By fools in old-style hats and coats,
Who half the time were soppy-stern
And half at one another's throats.

8.   The Rise and Pop of the Prosecco Mum

Much has been made of Rishi Sunak being our first xennial Prime Minister (someone born between 1975 and 1983) – despite the irony that it will probably be xennials, crumbling under spiralling mortgage rates and childcare costs, who will kick him out in eighteen months' time. For as much as our politicians represent a generational change of gear it's the voters, as we know, who exemplify the real tide of change.

Pollsters and political strategists love to fixate on sub-categories of swing voters that represent enough of a cultural shift and embody certain values that, if adequately appealed to, can push the electoral result definitively either way.

Back in the eighties there was 'Essex man', the aspirational and increasingly affluent working class type to whom Thatcherite policies of sound money, low taxation, and home ownership appealed. In the nineties, Tony Blair set out to win the affections of the voter known as 'Mondeo man': precisely those who had switched to the Tories under Thatcher and needed convincing to vote for New Labour. More recently, 'Workington man' was coined to describe working-class, non-graduate, pro-Brexit males and, ultimately, Conservative voters who guaranteed those critical red wall (traditional Labour) seats in 2019.

Historically, this has been a male-centric exercise, but floating female voters have been loosely drawn, too. In the nineties, 'Worcester woman' was used to describe a midlife woman in the Midlands whose reportedly consumerist values and a vague understanding of politics meant they were particularly susceptible to New Labour spin. For the critical 2010 election, Tory pollsters identified *Holby City* woman as someone who worked in the public sector but whose loose attachment to Labour and belief in tight fiscal discipline at home and in government translated in a swing to the Tories.

Floating voter caricatures are certainly crude and often pejorative and may have served merely as a convenient shorthand for the

Westminster commentariat; nonetheless they do have the capacity to reveal fundamental truths about how society (and yes, politics) is evolving.

In 2023, another important sub-group is emerging, one that symbolises the latest societal shift, a figure instantly recognisable in our workplaces, homes, and on our feeds, and whom politicians ignore at their peril: Prosecco mums.

But who is 'Prosecco mum'? In short, they are more Hunsnet than Mumsnet. You would be right in thinking they are xennial mothers who favour a certain Italian sparkling wine. One in-depth analysis of the Prosecco consumer from 2018 identified that forty-one per cent were graduates, eighty-one per cent lived with their partner or children, and the majority – fifty-two per cent – lived in the south of England. But that only tells half the story, for it is in the history of their favoured tipple that the legitimate political frustrations of these women are revealed.

The UK is the largest market in the world for Prosecco, importing a staggering 131 million bottles a year, which collectively makes up a third of the world's consumption. But it was not always so. Crucially, the rise of Prosecco coincided with the 2008 financial crisis, when it was marketed as a cheap but perfectly acceptable alternative to Champagne. It was '*bougee* on a budget' and one that specifically appealed to the xennial demographic who entered adulthood just as the world entered the deepest recession since the Second World War.

Xennial women had spent their youth downing Smirnoff Ice and Bacardi Breezers and thus were the first generation of women for whom alcohol consumption was socially encouraged, and they were as vigorously marketed to as young men. The ladette binge-drinking culture (think Zoe Ball and Sarah Cox before they settled into Radio 2) dominated our education years, followed by the aspirational *Cosmopolitan* and *Sex and the City* glamour that propelled our early working lives. Xennials coming of age symbolised an increasing equalisation of the sexes, a delaying of the traditional responsibilities of adulthood, and greater female financial independence. The drinks companies merely sought to capitalise on it all.

In the words of Professor Carol Emslie, there was a 'move away from sexualising women to sell alcohol to men towards alcohol brands trying to align their products with sophistication, women's empowerment, and with female friendship' – a point which she believes 'is really straight out of the tobacco industry playbook', a reference to when cigarette companies started aligning with the women's lib movement in the sixties to attract a new breed of liberated female smokers.

This 'pinking' of the alcohol market for xennial women reached new heights as they reached the next stage in life: motherhood. And so the social phenomenon of 'Prosecco mum' was born, one where 'wine o'clock' was promoted as 'Mummy's time out' from the exhaustive and relentless pressures of parenthood, complete with italic fonts and cheeky mum memes. As Canadian writer Ann Dowsett Johnston, author of *Drink: The Intimate Relationship Between Women and Alcohol*, surmised, 'Wine has become the code for "I deserve it, parenting is hard, I need to decompress."'

That Prosecco became a means of self-care and alleviation from the stresses of motherhood was no great leap from how spirits and beer had been historically marketed to men as a source of relaxation and reward at the end of the working day. Except of course, these women were both working and mothering and living in a twenty-first-century digital world where the ability to switch off became almost impossible.

For Prosecco mums their favourite fizz has also come to symbolise something more profound: an escape from the daily grind, a crucial and soothing reminder of life before motherhood, and a means of connecting with our younger selves; the immediate reawakening of individual freedom that comes from pouring something for yourself as you break from serving someone else. As Lisa Jacobson, an associate history professor at the University of California, Santa Barbara, states, 'It allows women to embrace their identity as mothers, while also refusing to be solely defined by that role.' This is critical for the generation who had children much later than their mothers and had literally decades of forming their identities before they had children (and yes, with much of that sense of self forged around alcohol).

But as much as the Prosecco mum delights in nostalgia for her youth, her very real and legitimate frustrations cannot be ignored. The pandemic awakened her sense of injustice as she morphed into a teacher and found herself fighting for the time and space to work. The bitterness of that experience has lingered and only intensified amid the cost-of-living crisis and spiralling mortgage costs. Her anger tends to resurface at the end of each month as she sees most of her wages go on childcare. She is exhausted, too, by a flexible working model that on the surface appears more malleable to mothering but in reality stretches her to breaking point. And let's not forget the constant guilt she feels while parenting in a culture that requires you to be constantly connected, stimulating, and present with your child – and to post about it regularly. Then there's the sense of dread she feels when she remembers that caring for her children will soon be replaced with caring for her ageing parents in a society where there is little state provision. Prosecco mum may not be overtly political but she is becoming more and more politicised.

Is it any wonder then that Prosecco mums have become more left-wing later in life? Rather than becoming more conservative with age, they are increasingly siding with the Labour Party and in doing so represent a significant break with female voting patterns of the last one hundred years. It used to be that the majority of women voted Conservative with more men tending to vote Labour, even though the gender gap was relatively small. Up until 2010 there was no major discernible difference in how men and women voted, but from 2015 onwards the gender gap in voting patterns started widening, with women under forty-five in particular tending to side with Labour. Thirty-seven per cent of women voted for Jeremy Corbyn in the last election, compared with just twenty-nine per cent of men. That the Tories have a 'women problem' is undeniable, but can Labour confidently claim that they have the Prosecco mum vote in the bag, especially with an electoral pitting of feminists vs trans-rights making things even harder for the Party?

The demographic that grew up with girl power are increasingly feeling powerless, not in respect of their stature, status, or life choices, as these have never been more validated, but rather in terms of the practical, economic, and social burdens of working motherhood. The double life may have become more socially acceptable since our mothers' day, but it arguably comes with higher expectations, financial necessities, and greater complications. Prosecco mums may be increasingly independent but are also increasingly worried and therefore increasingly politically important. So, if Tony Blair could embody the hopes and dreams of Mondeo man back in the mid-nineties, who today represents Prosecco mum? As images go, neither teetotal 'Dishy' Rishi nor 'Special K' Starmer really chime. A recent picture published of Angela Rayner in the DJ booth at a gig in Manchester cracking out N-Trance's *Set You Free*, on the other hand? Classic Prosecco mum vibes.

Chapter 3
Generations as Citizens

1. Why The Young Are Capitalists for Whom Capitalism Isn't Working
(*The Telegraph*, 29 January 2018)

Sometimes a narrative emerges in politics that becomes entrenched as conventional wisdom and seemingly immune from evidence to the contrary. One such misconception is Labour's 'youthquake'.

It has been taken as gospel since the election (2016) that anyone under thirty-five sits somewhere on the socialist spectrum. The assumption is that the millennials (those born after 1981) were driven into the open arms of Jeremy Corbyn at the election by the weight of tuition fee debt, soaring rents, and a lack of savings.

Tory campaign headquarters has been in a flap ever since, fretting about how Conservatives can win over a generation under Corbyn's spell; one that appears to subscribe to Labour's retro promises and that has a very low opinion of capitalism.

But now, according to the latest British Election Study report, which is the key tracker of changing trends since 1964, it appears that the youthquake is a myth[106]; the increase in millennial turnout at the election was minimal and their swing to Labour was only marginally significant.

This corrective should come as no surprise if you examine the values and behaviour of millennials, which are more in tune with the right than the left. In contrast to previous generations, millennials have fewer expectations of their employers (partly because they do not expect to be there beyond five years) and have been conditioned to have fewer expectations of the state in terms of education, welfare, and retirement.

They do, however, have greater expectations of the market. They are the first generation truly to define themselves by what they consume rather than by what they produce. They are highly individualistic and materialistic (this is not a disparaging term but, in fact, how millennials describe themselves according to Ipsos

MORI[107]). They have, knowingly or otherwise, absorbed the language of the market to such an extent that they now see themselves as a brand, managing their online PR on an hourly basis and always looking for new status updates.

So, for an accurate insight into this generation, political parties should look not to Momentum rallies or cushion-filled 'safe-spaces', but to the hundreds of entrepreneur societies that are thriving on UK campuses. Entrepreneurialism is the new rock 'n' roll, start-ups are the new bands, and disruption is their anthem – trends that are unsurprising given that this generation has grown up with the world's information and markets in their pockets.

This ethos has carried into employment, with many graduates having a 'side-hustle' – be it selling clothes online or tutoring while keeping down a full-time job. The recession has made them angry, but also resourceful.

So, what can the Tories do to win over millennials?

1. Nationalisation vs Privatisation
In the eighties, nationalisation was a point of ideological difference for voters – and it still is for politicians. For the public, however, this is no longer an ideological debate. It is a debate that hinges purely on frustrated consumer experience, especially for the young, who are the most sophisticated consumers in history – always ready to call out malpractice, hypocrisy, and poor service.

That is why the majority of under-24s (sixty-three per cent) support nationalising the railways. It isn't because they are Marxists, devoted to statist solutions and the taste of a stale British Rail sandwich – it's because they are infuriated by rip-off prices and bad service. Likewise with the postal service: sixty-five per cent of young people believe that Royal Mail should be nationalised[108].

For the party that understands this, however, there is a real political dividend: for millennials frustration in this area is shared by large numbers of over-65s. The issue has cross-generation cut-through.

2. Tuition Fees

This too is not an ideological issue, but a value-for-money issue. Some forty-eight per cent of graduates are not securing graduate-level jobs six months after leaving university[109]. No wonder then that school-leavers are wondering whether to go to university at all, while existing undergraduates are demanding a better service.

Academics now complain about over-demanding students, but the reality is that the power dynamic within universities has changed. You only have to see the adverts on the Tube to know that higher education is now a buyers' market and students see themselves as customers. It's not millennials who have to change – universities and political parties must react.

3. Housing and the NHS

Are millennials really fed up with the home-owning democracy, or is it that they are frustrated that they cannot own homes in this democracy? In reality, they do not want to do away with the notion of private property, but some twenty-six per cent of under-34s still live at home[110]. The Chancellor's Budget giveaway on stamp duty last November did little to alleviate their concerns; only thirty-six per cent of millennials believe that it would make homes more affordable, while twenty-nine per cent said it wouldn't make a difference.

Interestingly, young people (along with older voters) responded better to Philip Hammond's commitment to additional spending on the NHS than to the two policies specifically designed for them (the free railcard and the stamp duty cut), but this too should come as no surprise. And as millennials gain more direct experience of the NHS, through having children or caring for elderly relatives, this concern and connection with a nationalised health service can only grow.

So, it turns out that the crucial reason why Labour captured young votes is that they tapped into millennial consumer frustrations, not their innate socialist leanings. From an early age, millennials have been primed for the market but, growing up as they did in the longest consumer boom in history, they were also guaranteed to be frustrated, given that they entered adulthood during the longest recession in history.

The policy response to the financial crash, namely QE, has accentuated the distance between young people and the asset-owning class by inflating property, stocks, and asset values. And while millennials may be fundraisers, crowdsourcers, and spenders, they are not savers.

A combination of low wages, declining disposable incomes, high rents, and consumerism has meant that an entire generation is unable to perform this crucial behavioural function – buying a home – in a capitalist economy. They are capitalists for whom capitalism is not working.

4. The Environmentalist Attitude
Millennials' negative attitude towards the market has also been shaped by the culture of environmentalism, tech disruption, and the recent history of corporate misdemeanours that has made them particularly hostile towards corporate capitalism and big business.

The current Carillion fiasco is the latest example of a major turn-off: young people do not want to work for such companies, they don't want to buy from them, and they don't want the state to be in cahoots with them. This is the crucial distinction: millennials are aspirational, market-orientated consumers to their core, but capitalism is a dirty word and 'neoliberalism' is their favoured term of abuse.

However hypocritical it may be, millennials have been wired to embrace the hippy capitalism of Californian tech start-ups and to reject the moral market capitalism of Margaret Thatcher. David Cameron's 'Big Society', by contrast, actually has some cut-through with this generation; volunteering is not just a social obligation for millennials but a source of fulfilment, identity, and often a route into employment.

It will therefore take a lot more than a few policy sweeteners from the Chancellor or market-orientated speeches by the Prime Minister to win over millennial voters. Lazily labelling them 'socialists' or referencing the seventies or Venezuela won't gain much traction either.

At the last election, Corbyn benefited from stoking intergenerational tensions, but it is wrong to assume he had all the answers. Millennials are known for having no loyalty to brands and the same is probably true in politics. Put simply, they have greater allegiance to their phone tariff (which is to say, not much) than to any political party.

5. Future Demographics
One last crucial factor is that the millennials are growing up. The future is increasingly looking female and one of the most important voter groups in the next election will be millennial mothers. The majority of young women voted for Corbyn at the last election but the Tories have the potential to tap into their aspirations and concerns as they enter motherhood.

Just as the hippies of the sixties became the yuppies of the eighties, when it comes to the youth vote Labour should not be complacent — nor should the Tories feel that the game is up.

2. The Impact of Covid on Generation Alpha
(*UnHerd*, 9 November 2020)

Back when the first lockdown was lifted, and we entertained friends for the first time, my three-year-old son ran to the front door and shouted, 'Look Mummy, real people!' A few months feels like a few years to a toddler and my son hadn't played with someone his age since restrictions had set in.

We have heard a great deal about the impact of lockdown on new mothers and teenagers, but what about what it has done — and is doing — to younger children? Toddlers are, of course, endlessly adaptable, but they are also malleable: their experiences can have life-long consequences. The 'Babies In Lockdown' report[111], commissioned by three leading parenting groups and published in August, concluded that 'the pandemic will cast a long shadow', pointing to the fact that, just when they are meant to be building their social skills, emotional intelligence, and confidence, children have been prevented from properly engaging with the world. They desperately need routine but now, only a couple of months after things started getting back to normal, life has been disrupted again by this second lockdown.

I've definitely noticed little changes in my son's behaviour over the past month; largely harmless, they reveal the imprint of this pandemic on his still-emerging character. He puts on his mask when he plays shops and now scrubs his hands with a nailbrush, talking about germs. I once assumed it was impossible to impose hygiene standards and social distancing rules on toddlers, but as Natasha Rawdon-Rego, founder of Wimbledon's Oak Nursery, attests, her children have adapted — perhaps too well. 'It is almost like they police each other,' she says. The physical freedom of being a toddler is being restrained and they are becoming enthusiastic enforcers. One friend's toddler will protest when she sees crowds on TV, or people hugging, while another arranges her dolls into small groups so they are appropriately spaced. When organisations such as the Beavers issue Covid codes of conduct for children aged six to sign, it's surely time to question the value and legitimacy of it all.

In many ways, these new rules are much worse than the 'stranger danger' parental paranoia of yesteryear: we are now telling kids not to physically engage with people they actually know. My three-year-old is a potential 'superspreader' and his grandparents are potential victims. But how different and more challenging would this pandemic have been if it had been the other way round, with children in the vulnerable category needing to be shielded? That was precisely the case with the polio epidemic in the first half of the twentieth century. Playgrounds were shut, swimming pools were closed, and social distancing rules were put in place, especially in middle-class areas (it was found that working-class kids living in less sanitary conditions were actually more immune). Did the fear and restrictions scar baby boomers for life? Not really: most not directly touched by that epidemic can barely remember it.

All this suggests we need not fixate on the impact new societal rules are having on kids. Although it won't convince the Covid-sceptics, evidence from Asia points to the fact that mask-wearing can actually have a positive effect on a child's communication skills, because it makes them more perceptive of eye and facial expressions[112].

More important than any social rules, though, is what is going on in the home. As Philippa Perry, psychotherapist and author of *The Book You Wish Your Parents Had Read*, tells me, 'The greatest shaper of a child will be their environment and the mood of their parents, so they will pick up on what is going on at home.' She adds, 'Whether that is more lovely togetherness and family time and more attention, or more worry, fretfulness, and panic, they'll take in whatever is going on like a sponge and it will be a formative experience.'

With everyone confined to their homes, lockdown has revealed socioeconomic disparities like nothing else. Quality internet connection for schoolwork or a garden for exercise have become key social dividers. Investigations by academics at Oxford Brookes have shown the unsurprisingly detrimental impact the closure of free public spaces such as playgrounds and libraries has had on those families without books or a garden[113]. They also found that toddlers from low-income families ended up having higher daily screen use than those from wealthier families. But could this be a blip we all recover from?

The youngest generation have been dubbed 'coronnials'; born in the time of the Corona virus to millennial parents, usually into dual-income households. The defining characteristic of coronnials will not be their high standards of hygiene — or even the disruption of schoolwork — but their response to the major and lasting shift in their parents' working patterns. Those children whose parents are able to work from home will end up seeing far more of Mum and Dad than any other generation before them. 'For a lot of parents who work full time I think this has been a real opportunity,' observed Rawdon-Rego, speaking of her families in firmly middle-class Wimbledon. 'During lockdown on-line nursery, I went round the circle and asked if anyone wanted to share how they felt and one boy put his hand up. I asked him how he felt and he said, "Happy, because my daddy doesn't have to go to work anymore."'

So many parents who have worked from home feel that they have been gifted time, which largely explains why they are loath to return to the office. The length of this pandemic also means that new habits and new schedules are forming that are unlikely to be reversed when we return to 'normal', whenever and whatever that looks like.

Covid has also momentarily paused the incessant, activity-driven parenting common among middle-class millennials, who have been encouraged to think that family time has to be memorable, productive, and worthwhile. In perhaps a sign of the times, the Hoop app — which offers personalised lists of family activities and which had been downloaded by 1.5 million families in the UK — went out of business during lockdown and does not look likely to return. Perhaps parents have realised that all those toddler raves, samba dancing, Brazilian drumming, and coding camps made for great social media posts, but in reality were exhausting and expensive. Fresh air, independent play, and occasional boredom are just as rewarding.

But those whose parents are unable to work from home — which in towns like Barnsley means eight out of ten workers[114] — are bound to suffer disproportionately. Services that provide childcare have been restricted or closed, while parents have been unable to lean on friends and family who might ordinarily step in to help. The impact of the stress caused by this situation should not be underestimated: an NSPCC report[115] on the risk of child maltreatment in lockdown found that 'increase in stressors to parents and care givers' could 'increase the risk of physical, emotional, and domestic abuse' as well as neglect and online harm.

And for those children for whom home is not safe, lockdown has been a terrible experience. Social workers dreaded the closure of schools back in March because of the crucial structure they provide for vulnerable children. One Met police officer in Hackney tells me that in 'normal times' cases relating to minors are normally referrals from social workers or schools, but under lockdown his unit saw an increasing number of children ringing 999 themselves (which inevitably meant theirs were emergencies or at least very serious cases). Meanwhile, social workers are finding that social distancing is compromising their work: it is very difficult to talk to a child about potential abuse or a care plan over video or in a mask.

Fortunately, schools have remained open since the second lockdown kicked in. However, other institutions are once again threatened, meaning that children will yet again be confined to home. More time spent together as a family will be the force that shapes this generation, for better or worse. Fundamentally, there will be a divide, more evident and visible as time goes on, between children whose family structures nurtured them during the great pandemic and those whose circumstances exacerbated the crisis and compounded their disadvantages.

3. When the Market and State Fail, the Family Steps In
(*UnHerd*, 1 December 2020)

Economic conditions have made adults, young and old, more dependent on their relatives

Throughout the course of this pandemic, the Government has wielded many a blunt instrument, of which Heath Secretary Matt Hancock's '**Don't kill your gran**' message[116] was perhaps the bluntest. Yet this slogan, directed at young superspreaders, spoke to a little remarked on truth about British life in the twenty-first century: family life is on the up, and stronger than ever.

This runs counter to the long-held and entrenched narrative that in Britain family is in decline. Its preservation was a cause for moral conservatives, from Mary Whitehouse to Margaret Thatcher, in the final three decades of the twentieth century, worried that the permissive sixties had triggered a loosening of values and the breakdown of the family, with rising levels of divorce and teen pregnancy.

But tell anyone under twenty-five of the moral battles of the eighties and they may well switch off, so alien is it to their experience. In fact, contrary to fears that the family would wither, the opposite has happened over the past twenty years, with a quiet revolution taking place in Britain's homes. Not only has there been a massive decrease in teenage pregnancy[117] along with a drop in divorce rates[118] (as prayed for by social conservatives), but a more fundamental strengthening of the family has also taken place.

As the state has withdrawn and the housing market has become dysfunctional, more and more of us have invested in the family, creating a new culture of dependency between parent and offspring.

Britain has often been contrasted with its Mediterranean counterparts and their trestle tables full of family. We Anglo-Saxons, supposedly, are inherently more individualistic — more likely to strike out on our own and move far from home. Historically that has been the case, but in fact, **forty per cent** of children starting primary school live fewer than fifteen minutes away from their maternal grandparents[119]. And as the cost of nursery and childminding has rocketed, grandparents have become increasingly valuable, saving parents an estimated **£16 billion** by providing informal childcare[120]. During lockdown, thousands of dual-income couples struggled to care for their children without the support of now-isolated grandparents, revealing how increasingly dependent we are on our relatives.

In recent years, Britain has mirrored the rest of the Western world in shifting its economic model from the nuclear to the extended family. A **third of UK households** — around nine million in total — are now multigenerational[121] (classified as more than one adult generation living under one roof). 'Grannexes', to use the neologism, are increasingly popular; some **five per cent of UK households** are already equipped with such a space, and an additional seven per cent say they plan to add one[122]. The reciprocal benefits are obvious, and if you had space for a pram, why not a wheelchair?

For an ageing society, filial responsibility is vital; in a pandemic, of course, it may prove fatal. One **thread of research** by demographers at Oxford suggests that early death rates were much higher in those countries that have a large proportion of multigenerational homes[123]. It is thought to be one reason why we have seen higher than average infection rates among Asian communities.

Politicians have been scratching their heads for the past decade trying to fix the social care crisis and the scale of the cost is daunting, but most elderly care comes not from private or state organisations but from families themselves — **worth an estimated £57 billion** in time and money[124]. The majority of those carers are of course women — daughters and daughters-in-law — and **one-fifth** expects to have to leave jobs to care for an adult relative[125]. Some companies have started offering paid leave for those with such responsibilities, and eventually the state will begrudgingly have to catch up.

But the contemporary boom in family values is better understood in our treatment of the young rather than the old. The 'boomerang' children phenomenon — in which adult offspring remain in the family home well into adulthood — may reflect thirtysomething economic woes, but it is also testimony to the strength of familial relations. Britain is not unique in this respect. In Italy, **seventy-three per cent of male eighteen to thirty-four-year-olds** still live at home[126] (known as *mammoni* – 'mama's boys'), while in South Korea they are called 'kangaroos' – forever in their parents' pockets.

That younger generation are also proving far more conventional than their predecessors. **According to the ONS,** divorce rates for young people are at their lowest rate since 1973, while divorce is increasing for older people[127]. And although young people also have lower marriage rates to start with, it remains a popular institution, nowhere more so than among same-sex couples.

The children of those marriages also see a lot more of their parents, especially their fathers, reflecting the changing nature of parental commitment over the past forty years. As the fertility rate has halved since 1960, so this has led to greater investment in our children. In 2012, mothers spent nearly an hour more each day looking after their kids than they did in 1965[128], despite the fact that the majority was now working. Fathers also saw a rise, with time spent with their children increasing from sixteen minutes a day to fifty-nine. A 2015 **study by the University of Texas** found that same-sex couples actually spent the most time with their kids, with gay dads spending as much time parenting as straight mums, and twice as much time as heterosexual fathers[129].

We are giving our kids not only more time but also more money. To have a child today is a thirty-year financial commitment, as many older people are now learning: **and parents now expect to be supporting their kids until they're twenty-nine**[130] (and even that might be optimistic). Parents are putting twice as much into their kids' living costs as they are their own future retirement funds, perhaps assuming that it will all be paid back, one way or another.

These days, university open days are populated with over-excited parents, and tutors direct their 'sales pitch' mostly at the grown-ups (universities know who their real customers are). Even employers are being forced to engage with Mum and Dad: in 2018, more than 20,000 parents took part in LinkedIn's 'take your parents to work day' initiative[131]; a strange modern twist on an older tradition.

What is most strikingly conservative is how well all the generations get along. Teenage rebellion is no more: Generation Z are more likely to see their parents as friends than as enemies, while a quarter of girls have been clubbing with their mums[132], something that would have been the stuff of nightmares to children of the eighties. And although the 18-30 holiday market has struggled, the 18-70 market is booming: seventy-nine per cent of twenty to thirty-year-olds in the UK have taken a multigenerational holiday while one-fifth say they prefer holidaying with their parents than with their mates[133].

But how many would go on such holidays with their parents if they were the ones paying? Families may enjoy hanging out more than they used to, but the trigger for this shift is changing economics, not changing values. Affluent millennials have been financially dependent on their parents like no other generation before them — for an education, a house deposit, a wedding, support with childcare, and the family crash pad if it all goes wrong. The 'Bank of Mum and Dad' is now equivalent to the ninth largest mortgage lender in the UK[134]. But how long can parents keep giving their kids so much? The next generation doesn't have anything like their parents' wealth.

The real divide within the under-40s demographic lies not between graduates and non-graduates but between those who can rely on the parental safety net and those who can't. This is the new dependency culture: one where aspiration and opportunity is conditional on family support and there is little the market or the state can do to level the playing field.

Much of what the social conservatives of the eighties craved has happened; and yet everything they said about the family was wrong. The reinvestment in the family unit is not down to the reinforcement of moral or religious responsibilities, but economic interdependence. Family values, especially for the young, means more parental support than ever — with the expectation that they'll take filial responsibilities seriously as our society ages. Both now and in the future, relatives simply cannot afford to live apart. The family has become society's guarantor, which even in a global pandemic is both a curse and a source of relief.

4. Why Gen Z's Education Won't Stop at Graduation
(*The Telegraph*, 18 December 2020)

University at eighteen used to be a rite of passage but younger generations will discover that life-long learning defines them instead

'I want to study history because history is knowledge and knowledge is power.' That was the rather arrogant opening line of my UCAS personal statement back in 1998. I may have written it twenty-two years ago, but I can well remember the intense pressure I felt (enhanced by well-intentioned parental encouragement) as I justified and summarised the first eighteen years of my existence into 500 words.

I didn't know then that this degree would be the first of three (accompanied by a short stint as a university lecturer) and that my education and career would, like most of my millennial generation, be a meandering wander of fancy and desperation rather than a linear destination.

As the latest crop of students pen their UCAS forms and weigh up their options, it may be worth considering just how the point, purpose, and value of a degree has changed and what Gen Z (and their parents) need to consider as they start the third stage of their educational journey.

Millennials were told that if you did well in school and got a decent degree you would be set up for life. But that promise has been found wanting.

Non-graduate Roles
As degrees became universal, they became devalued (just as governments hiked up the cost of getting one) and education ceased to be a secure route to social mobility. Today, twenty-eight per cent of graduates in the UK are in non-graduate roles[135]; double the average percentage among OECD countries.

Visit any university campus in the UK and you will realise that today's graduates are in a global graduate race, so international is the student base. But there is a problem brewing: China produces eight million graduates every year[136] and yet its graduates are four times more likely to be unemployed than manual workers.

In India, 16.3 per cent of graduates are unemployed (the highest of any group)[137]. The global graduate race is already turning into widespread global graduate dissatisfaction. That is not to say that there is no point in getting a degree, but rather stresses that a degree is not for everyone, that the switch from classroom to lecture hall is not inevitable, and that other options are available.

Thankfully, there are signs that this is already happening, with Gen Z seeking to learn from their millennial predecessors, even if parents and teachers tend to be still set in the degree mindset.

Employers have long seen the advantages of hiring school-leavers who often prove to be more committed and loyal employees than graduates. Many too are seeing the advantages of scrapping a degree requirement for certain roles, just as Penguin did in 2016[138]. Apprenticeships too are getting a much-needed rebrand beyond the blue-collar stereotype; roles in technology are especially coveted and seen as a quicker route into the tech sector than a degree, where the teaching content often lags behind industry.

For those for whom a degree is the desired route, consider that this may well be the first of many. In this age of generalists, it pays to have specific knowledge or skills: postgraduates now earn forty per cent more than graduates[139]. When more and more of us have a degree, it makes sense (albeit expensive sense) to have two.

Generation Z, more than any other generation, will be most exposed to artificial intelligence (AI) infiltrating the workplace and rendering certain professional skills redundant.

It is unlikely that Gen Z will be done with education at eighteen or twenty-one; they will need to be constantly up-skilling throughout their careers to stay agile, relevant, and employable. It has been estimated that this generation, due to the pressures of technology, the wish for personal fulfilment, and desire for diversity, will work for seventeen different employers over the course of their working lives and have five different careers[140]. That may seem a rather ridiculous prediction, but consider my own familial example: my mother, a baby boomer, worked for one company for fifty-five years; I, as a millennial, will have had three different careers before I am forty. Education, and not just knowledge gained on campus, will be a core part of Generation Z's career trajectory.

So let's not fixate on one UCAS form or even one degree. University acceptance may be a nice status update for parents and provide good stats for schools, but it is not a destination in itself; it is rather the beginning of a long, professional, educational journey that may well last decades.

I have often heard older generations talk about their degrees (even if it was gained decades ago) in the present and personal tense: 'I am a geographer' or 'I am a classicist'. Their sons or daughters would never say such a thing: it's as if they already know that their degree won't define them in the same way.

5. When Did it Become So Tough to Be Young?
(Published: 19 March 2021)

Youth is supposed to be about being reckless and carefree . . . instead today's young are serious, sober, and stressed.

'Everybody's youth is a dream, a form of chemical madness,' wrote F. Scott Fitzgerald. He would become the chronicler of the Lost Generation; those who survived the First World War, loosened their corsets and morals and embraced the heady Jazz Age. Fitzgerald himself was obsessed with youth – so much so that he mourned turning thirty.

'Youth is wasted on the young,' so the axiom goes, but does this saying still ring true? 'I'm glad I was young when I was' is what most people over forty say these days, no doubt relieved that they did not have to endure its modern version of tech overload, social media pressures, financial instability, debt, and poor job prospects, to say nothing of formative years disrupted by a pandemic. So what has changed? The notion of carefree adolescence and early adulthood were invented in the twentieth century, but is it disappearing in the twenty-first?

A Structured Millennial Childhood
Thinking back, it is depressing how much of my childhood was geared towards being productive; exams of course, but also all those extra-curricular activities – Duke of Edinburgh Awards, internships – anything to flesh out that CV. It was all so serious and scheduled and a marked contrast to my baby boomer parents. My mother passed the eleven-plus but left school at sixteen, while my father made it to art school but was kicked out, having been deemed too non-conformist even for the   Slade in the sixties.

Millennials' economic disadvantages are well known: we are the first generation to be worse off than our parents. But it is actually our frustrations and dashed hopes that define us. We grew up being told by teachers, parents, and society that if we worked hard the rewards would be forthcoming. Instead, our first decades in work have been characterised by poor pay, job insecurity, and fewer opportunities than we'd come to expect. Millennial disaffection with housing is nothing compared to our frustrations over what was essentially the mis-selling of a degree as a guaranteed path to prosperity and mobility. And this is a global problem: graduate underemployment is as much of an issue in China and India as it is in the West. Remember though, that these are the complaints of those who 'succeeded' in education; the struggles of those who did not are far, far worse.

Blame it on the Boomers?
I can almost hear the collective groan from older generations as they read this lament. And yet they are a key part of this tale. Our parents the baby boomers were the original architects of modern youth culture: 1968 'n' all that. The symbols, rituals, behaviours, and expectations of youth – even its uniform of jeans and trainers – were popularised and to a large degree invented by the boomers. They were more affluent and better educated than any generation before them. Their parents' youth was synonymous with sacrifice during the war and the generation after them were bound by fifties conformity and silence (so much so they became known as 'the silent generation'). Boomers, on the other hand, were associated with rebellion and individualism; leading journalist Tom Wolfe famously dubbed them the 'Me' generation.

What actually defined this generation though was their clout. The term 'baby boom', first coined in the forties, soon came to refer to the economic as well as the demographic windfall associated with that generation. When boomers were teenagers, the ad men of Madison Avenue fell over themselves to cater to the new adolescent experience. When boomers were in their twenties, the media and politics clapped to their beat. Boomers were talked about as a collective generation, said to be united by age and time rather than gender, race, or class. Boomers' delayed entry into adulthood was for the most part a time of freedom and experimentation. Believe them when they say those were the best days of their lives.

Sixties Nostalgia
Boomer nostalgia and celebration of their youth began pretty much as soon as the party was over. The first decade anniversary of hippy

music festival Woodstock was commemorated in 1979, and again in 1989. 'I don't want to be singing "Satisfaction" when I'm forty,' Mick Jagger once said, and yet, still touring today, he's lionised rather than ridiculed for it. In the nineties, *Absolutely Fabulous* flipped the parent-child dynamic on its head, but it was only funny because it mocked the unique boomer obsession with their own youth. Even today the original iconoclasts find it hard to be cast as traditionalists and during this pandemic have struggled to be cast as vulnerable. Joanna Lumley of *Ab Fab* fame told a newspaper recently that she refused to consider herself as such.

But the boomers' transition into adulthood was far from easy and echoed millennial struggles. A self-help industry flowered in the seventies to ease their growing pains. Works such as *What Colour Is Your Parachute?*, *Your Erroneous Zones*, and *How to Be Your Own Best Friend* dominated the bestsellers' list; the latter offering advice on 'how to give up childhood, accept yourself and your own maturity and deal with life on your own two feet' (sound familiar, millennials?).

As the boomers turned thirty, they faced record inflation (in 1980 in the UK it was twenty per cent), rising youth unemployment, and declining wages, notably among college graduates. A report by the United States Treasury in 1980 gave a rather dismal projection that baby boomers would never achieve the relative economic success of the generation before or after them. The *New York Times* wrote of a 'generational malaise of haunting frustrations, anxiety, and depression'. [141]

Then along came Thatcher and Reagan and the hippies of the sixties transformed into the yuppies of the eighties. In the words of one generational biographer, boomers' lives became less about 'improving society, more about improving themselves.' And, their kids, like their homes, became an extension of this status update.

Millennials Trapped in the Boomer Straitjacket
For their millennial children, however, a late-twentieth-century childhood was a contradictory mix of fear and aspiration. 'Stranger danger' warnings, the AIDS epidemic and 9/11 punctuated a culture

where child-rearing was less about freedom and fun and more about structured play and learning resources. The latchkey kids of the seventies (so-called because of a carefree upbringing) morphed into helicopter parents of the nineties. Global literacy levels became as prominent as GDP to signpost national prowess. Parents began to obsess about school places. Girls, whose mothers had lived through the feminist movement, were encouraged to invest their future in education rather than the marriage market. It worked: they started to outshine boys at school and would eventually outnumber them at university.

'Blame it on the boomers' has become a common cultural trope, but actually their only fault is that there were so many of them. Their priorities have always been society's priorities – as babies, young adults, parents, and now pensioners (er, triple-lock anyone?). Their youthful experience defined them, but as parents they oversaw a new era of youth – being young became bloody hard work. And millennials have found it impossible to escape from the straitjackets their parents put them in; the studious path we were told to tread.

As much as we can blame them, the millennials' disadvantage also stems from being born in the wrong time: we're destined to be 'inbetweeners'. Just like Edwardians propping up the Victorian legacy, millennials have one foot in and one foot out of the twentieth century, hankering after a post-war story of aspiration and opportunity that is no longer a reality for most people. Contrast that with savvy Generation Z, who have no such hang-ups or delusions. They already outnumber millennials across the globe and are true twenty-first-century kids on the make. Their derogatory 'OK, boomer' meme conveys this distance and freedom; it's a proverbial rolling of the eyes to the last century and all its false promises.

Tech has robbed Gen Z of the innocence and experimentation of youth, but Gen Z youth are enslaved by other forces and have been compelled to mature much more quickly than previous generations. The debilitating effects of unregulated technology, a comparative culture, an exam-driven curriculum, fear of social shaming, and a reduced attention span are borne out in the mental health crisis among Gen Zers. Those factors also explain why they are so remarkably well behaved. Gen Z are not the victims of too much sex, drugs and rock 'n' roll, but rather too much parenting. Generational expert Jean Twenge has analysed how driving licence uptake, once the first passage into adulthood, has declined among Gen Z[142]. Why? Because there is little incentive when their parents are willing chauffeurs. Not only has it become harder to be young but there also isn't the same incentive to mature – and that has little to do with house prices.

The new generation of millennial parents – those with pre-schoolers now – are doing their best to learn from those mistakes. The popularity of forest nurseries and retro wooden toys suggest a desire to shield their offspring and preserve the wonder and innocence of childhood that was stolen from the iPhone generation. Watch as millennial parents over the next decade challenge the exam and degree-driven education system that failed them.

Today, our youthful experience may last well beyond Fitzgerald's cut-off point of thirty, and neither is it the 'chemical madness' that he once claimed it to be. Youth, as the boomers invented it, is no more. A twenty-first-century youth feels fraught with pressures: an expectation of direction, an expectation that you should be enjoying the ride, and an expectation that it will all be in vain. Millennials' sense of frustration and betrayal is palpable and will only intensify as we hit middle age with greater responsibilities in life, caring for parents as well as our kids. For now, the young play the new puritans, pitting themselves against the *bon viveur* boomers, but they may well be heading for one hell of a midlife crisis.

6. What Happens to Our Data When We Die?
(Published: 22 March 2022)

In an ageing society death is a growth industry, but it is taking on a different course in the twenty-first century – one for which we are woefully unprepared

When my father was in a hospice, in and out of consciousness, his neurological pathways would be sparked not by the familiar, the habitual, or even the new, but by flashes of a long-forgotten past. It was why I spent the last few weeks of his life, night after night, scanning old family photos and videos, tracking down old music hall songs his mother used to play on the piano, and TV Westerns that had transported him to another world as a kid (boomers are the TV generation after all). The closer to his childhood I could get, the more he seemed alive. Dying is often an infantilising process, but my father actively desired to return to his fifties boyhood existence. It was where he felt most at peace, least in pain. Admittedly, as someone desperate to make the most of those final days and hours, I was frustrated by my father's yearning to return to a time when those around him didn't even know him – but who was I to resent it?

My father can be said to have had a good death; slipping away, in search of nostalgia, surrounded by family. But perhaps his generation is the last for whom this elaborate process of data mining and effort to reconnect with a distant past will be necessary or even desired. The notion of me demanding to watch old episodes of *Neighbours* in my final days seems ludicrous, as does the idea of my kids struggling to track down evidence of my life should they or I wish to reminisce. My iPhone is already pinging me with that service, compiling ready-made mini-videos complete with sentimental music documenting my weekends, let alone my decades. Timehop and Facebook's 'On This Day' reminders thrust memories into my view even before they've had time to blur into memories in my mind. The algorithm constantly regurgitates life's showreel, creating a disorientated sense of time. But the accumulated data that is being gathered throughout our lives is ultimately leading to a new frontier for the digital age: our death will be disrupted by data as much as our lives have been.

Death in the late twentieth century was already on a different trajectory due to the decline of infant mortality, longer life expectancy and yes, the demise of religion, or more specifically, the declining belief in a Christian-expressed afterlife. However, it's been a slower process than we might think, for while traditional Christian sacraments of weddings and baptisms ceased to be the markers of status and security and went into steady decline from the sixties, church funerals persisted. 'Dust to dust, ashes to ashes' has turned out to be the resilient fag end of Christendom. But as the baby boomer generation begins to leave us, so their farewells are reflecting their generational tale as the first individualists in a gradually secularising world. My dad's burial, for example, took place in his own back garden, befitting the life experience of a late-twentieth-century cradle Christian; a cultural mashup of the King James Bible and the Sex Pistols' 'Anarchy in the UK'.

As assisted dying grows in social acceptance and becomes legal across the world – Spain, New Zealand, and Canada have all consented in the last two years – we may be in danger of overseeing the pressing issue on the horizon: the right to our data in the afterlife. Death is what trendspotters like to call 'a growth industry', not just because of ageing demographics, but also due to the accumulation of the data of the dead. Every day, approximately 8,000 Facebook users die[143].

Back in 2019, researchers at the Oxford Internet Institute calculated that profiles of the deceased would outnumber the living by 2050, rising to 4.9 billion 'dead' profiles by 2100[144]. Forget election tampering: Zuckerberg is set to become the Grim Reaper CEO of a mass digital graveyard. There is a certain irony that Meta, the company's new name, means 'dead' in Hebrew[145]. Perhaps Zuckerberg envisages the metaverse as the place where we are all reincarnated?

In growing recognition of this phenomenon all the major tech companies now have policies in place, but the data remains theirs, not yours. It's long been said that if a service is free then you are the product. Now comes a new caveat: whether you are alive or dead. If every business is now a tech business, then every tech business will very soon be in the death business. And the data of the dead will be as valuable as that of the living, particularly while there are no regulations in place. While irreligious Silicon Valley types have spent years trying to 'hack' ageing and prevent dying, we have begun to see a pivot where 'angel' investors see the dollar signs not in longevity but in digital reincarnation, where funerals begin to mirror a hackathon rather than a sacrament. You can hear the funding pitch now: 'Artificial intelligence can't just predict your behaviour; it can do something much more reliable and potentially more valuable: breathe life into you.' It's a fast-moving industry: NFT memorial stones are already selling in the metaverse, with links to individual's memorial halls and digital archives, while a media company in South Korea has pursued the unthinkable – bringing a mother's daughter back from the grave using virtual reality[146].

Social media operates on mining your data to sell you stuff. What could that mean in the age of a digital afterlife with AI and avatars? In a benign world, it could mean the ability to ask your mum's avatar for her old crumble recipe or enquire about her experience of the menopause. Many are predicting a warped future where holograms of the deceased give the eulogy at their own funeral, but we could potentially see something much worse: the monetisation of the deceased, where your mum's avatar pops up on your feed to sell you life insurance. We already have actors performing beyond the grave on our screens, so why not our deceased relatives selling us stuff on our social platforms?

Dystopian visions aside, we are heading into a world where digital wills and 'legacy contacts' will become the norm, and maybe a new death-bed test where you regret not the things you haven't done but the things you wish you hadn't posted.

But let's not dwell on what will be corrupted, better to ask what will be lost. Crumble recipes, family stories, and traditions operate because they are passed down, generation to generation, through the unreliable oral tradition, and like Chinese whispers, inevitably lose accuracy, gain embellishments, but retain emotional currency. Like all questions surrounding death, the real victims are always the living. My grief for my father was ultimately aided by the fact that I am not constantly reminded of his life in this modern world. Grief isn't just about coming to terms with the reality that someone has gone; it is also about understanding your place in life's great chain, and ultimately reconciling with the fact that life goes on. How disrupted would this process be if none of us were ever really allowed to check out of planet Earth? It is a common trope that tech has made us an angrier, more unforgiving, more divisive society, but technology could also give rise to an even greater psychological danger – that we could lose the ability, and the right, to let go.

7. Why Millennials Are Suffering Most
(Published: 5 April 2022)

I'm a geriatric millennial, which means I'm old enough to remember when the most controversial topic of debate was what we should put in the Millennium Dome. The answer, it turned out, was not much: a home planet section (inexplicably) sponsored by British Airways; the body zone, with a giant, amorphous sculpture that looked like an A-level imitation of a Henry Moore; and a faith zone that offended everyone and appealed to no one. That was back in 1999, when we weren't quite sure what we were celebrating or why (aside from a massive New Years' Eve party).

We like to misremember that period as one of prosperity and peace; the 'end of history', and a neat denouement to the destructive 'isms' that had ravaged the twentieth century. We now know it was in a fact a mere intermission: after Thatcher but before 9/11. It was when the 'third way' meant no way at all and we bathed in blissful ignorance of what the next millennium would hold.

Twenty-two years into the twenty-first century and the timeline is becoming clear: terrorism and 'techlash'; populism and pandemics; climate crises and China. Indeed, the twenty-first century's most pronounced feature right now seems to be its relentlessness. We talk of a 'permacrisis' and a new age of turbulence; our doomscrolling may be damaging, but it is justified. The Brexit deal was finally signed on 24 January 2020; just four days later the first cases of Covid were confirmed in the UK. Two years later, the Government finally announced the end of the pandemic restrictions, that same day Russia began its assault on Ukraine. These are not the inflated headlines of the twenty-four-hour news cycle, but events with consequence; the kind of stuff you will tell your kids and they won't believe and the kind of news that has scary historical parallels. Add into the mix the slow-mo car crash that is climate change and no wonder many of us say that global events are intensifying our anxiety.

Social media has not only forced us to constantly digest the news, but also to respond and react to it. Armed with our megaphones and whipped up into a frenzy by our echo chambers, a rigid tribalism on specific issues (Brexit, the vaccine, and other culture war flashpoints) takes hold; these issues – and where we stand on them – become our identifiers and supersede any overarching ideology that we or our ancestors subscribed to. We now have a firm list of no-go subjects at family gatherings and in our workplaces. While some go in search of fierce debate, others retreat into safe spaces, be it anonymity online or private group chats with fellow believers. The point is that the events themselves become immaterial: it's the position we take on them that is internalised.

For anyone over thirty-five, all of this is particularly disorientating because most of us continue to act, think, and speak like we are still in the twentieth century. We shudder in disbelief when we realise that 1980 is the same span of time away from 2022 as it is from 1939. We refuse to connect the dots of change and see the consequences, and instead fixate on a miscalculated understanding that the institutions and beliefs with which we grew up with still reign. The morbid truth is that it may take the death of the Queen for many of us to realise that the curtain has truly fallen on the last century.

I say *we*, but it is worth being specific because the age of turbulence has hit the millennial generation particularly hard; much harder than Gen Z, who cannot remember the twentieth century and are fully acclimatised (and best prepared) for the disruptions of the twenty-first, despite being mislabelled as snowflakes; much harder than Gen X who, with all this talk of nuclear annihilation, are rekindling vague childhood memories of the Cold War and whose view of the future is increasingly seen through the eyes of their Gen Z kids. And it's hit them much harder than even baby boomers, who have long been resigned to not recognising the modern world (even if they never stop vocalising their discontent). For millennials, as the restless inbetweeners with a foot in both centuries and now hitting early middle age, the disorientation is real.

We grew up during the longest consumer boom in history and, although we came of age in the deepest recession since the Second World War, we held on to the idea that the good times would return.

Like the Edwardians millennials are straitjacketed by the conventions of a former age, even though those trappings (tertiary education, mortgage, conventional career, even retirement) are becoming less and less relevant. We allow the false promises of the last century to define us in a way that Gen Z does not. Perhaps this uniquely millennial disposition reflects the overwhelming influence on us – both financial and ideological – of our baby boomer parents, the twentieth century's great demographic force. Or maybe it is because we ourselves are now parents, specifically of small children, a time when one's paranoia about the future is most pronounced.

It is also because we are hitting our forties. We emerged out of our Covid bunkers only to be confronted with the stark realisation that we are no longer young. But our age is just a number in all this; the real trigger is that Gen Zers have stolen the mic, and are directing much of their youthful ire and mockery towards us. Gen Z memes on our love of skinny jeans and side partings only serve to remind us of our displacement as the purveyors of youth culture. Millennials took the slow lane to adulthood and now it seems we're being fast-tracked to middle age. It is disorientating to hear a Gen Z talk excitedly about NFTs when we've only just reached credit card maturity; it is demoralising to hear Gen Z proudly pledge they are avoiding university when we have only just paid off our student loan. This evolution, from being the disrupters to the disrupted, is of course the natural order of things, but the problem is that millennials' time in the limelight was so fleeting. At some point between 2014 and 2019, millennials were the future. Now we have to deal with the discomforting feeling that we are already on the wrong side of history.

But as is so often the case, a weakness is ultimately a strength: we may be inbetweeners, but millennials also have the potential to be a bridge. As the 21st century progresses and the new world order comes into being, millennials will have a role to play as the 'elder statesman' in our workplaces, politics, and society at large over the next forty years. As the systems of AI mature, millennials may find themselves as the only ones talking about the value of privacy. As international alliances coalesce around new energy resources, we may well be the only ones who remember what liberal democracy supposedly stands for. As we rebuild communities, we may find ourselves the only ones who remember what a social democratic infrastructure looks like. As we build peer-to-peer information systems, we may be the ones promoting verifiers and gatekeepers. As Gen Z and subsequent generations ride a wave of innovation and change, we millennials may find our generational moment in being the bridge and the breaks. Forget all talk of the 'new normal', because the world is now on a different setting and the relentlessness is unlikely to stop. Buckle up, and welcome to the twenty-first century.

8. Boomer Grandparents v Millennial Parents
(Published: 19 June 2022)

Admit it, we've all done it: made snap judgements of others' parenting. But it takes a brave soul to vocalise it.

I have been called both a bad mother and a good mother by random members of the public. On one occasion, on a hot, packed Tube – the day of an England World Cup match no less – I and my then two-year-old son were engaged in quite a rough tussle with a Slinky. I was interrupted by a man who informed me that I was overstimulating my child and that it would be best if I left my son alone. My reaction was naturally incandescent rage. The man may have been right, but he didn't know the context: my father had just passed away, it was one week from my wedding, and I hadn't seen my son all day.

On another occasion, I was in a cafe playing 'guess which hand it's in' with the only suitable item in my handbag, a tampon, in order to distract my very hungry daughter while we waited for our order. A lady passed by and informed me how nice it was to see a mother entertaining her child with something other than a screen. Again, she was unaware of the context: my daughter had spent the morning in front of *Cocomelon* while I worked. It is worth pointing out that in both incidents this feedback on my parenting came from older people – probably parents, possibly now grandparents.

But far more often, such awkward exchanges are happening within families rather than between strangers. In a recent US poll, forty-three per cent of parents said they had been in conflict with grandparents over the parenting of their children. And many of those conflicts remain unresolved, with fifty-three per cent of grandparents refusing to change their approach even after a plea had been made.

In the UK, grandparents save families thousands per year by providing informal childcare and, with the rise of multi-generational living and millennial financial dependency on the Bank of Mum and Dad (a lot of which is spent directly on the grandchildren), the stage is set for an intergenerational collision in parenting priorities and styles. Nowhere is this clash more pronounced than in first and second-generation immigrant families where the economic power play may be less obvious, but the expectation of adhering to tradition is more intense.

So, what are the areas of dispute? It depends on which generation you speak to. According to one US survey, grandparents bemoaned the lack of parental discipline as well as displaying differing priorities on manners, respect and money. Grandparents overwhelmingly believed that parents gave their children too much power. According to parents though, forty per cent said that disagreements occurred because grandparents were too lenient on the child. They can't even agree on what they disagree on. Not all families, of course, experience such tensions, and I'm sure there are many who live in a harmonious, multi-generational bubble. For many though, the tussle can feel undermining and unresolvable on both sides. And quite often, it is the major source of intergenerational, predominantly female, tension within the family. But why is that so?

The reason is part personal, part social. Becoming a parent required, for me at least, the forging of a new identity and, given I was well into my thirties when I had my first child, it took me a couple of years to find my confidence and style. It certainly didn't happen the moment I got pregnant, or gave birth; it was probably only when I was faced with a recalcitrant toddler with his own voice and teeth. It is a fact rarely acknowledged that in this era of multi-faceted and fluid identities, motherhood too requires a transition, possibly constant transition, as your children grow. And because it is so intimately personal but so often on public display, it comes with an inevitable degree of defensiveness and quite often results in an unspoken yet real divide within the sisterhood. Put bluntly, any criticism or observation, however small, cuts deep.

And, as much as parenting is about nurturing the next generation, it also naturally prompts a reconciling with one's own childhood. Every parent seeks to learn from (even if they are doomed to repeat them) the mistakes of their parents. And this desire is particularly felt by the millennial generation who, for good or ill, have been nurtured in a culture of self-analysis and self-improvement. Yes, it may be optimistic, but millennials feel compelled to break negative intergenerational cycles more than any other generation before them.

The reason also lies in the new social context in which we are now operating. The twenty-first century parenting landscape of gender reveal parties, hypnobirthing, and 'sharenting' on social media is understandably incongruous to older generations. But then today's parents reflect in disbelief that doctors were once accepting of smoking during pregnancy and that parents used to put babies to sleep on their stomachs and were encouraged to train away left-handedness in their children. Is there an area that is more subject to changing advice and evolving trends than parenting?

Millennial parents are navigating challenges that their boomer counterparts did not have to contend with; principally twenty-four-hour hand-held interconnected tech. It's a burden they feel keenly: in a poll conducted before the pandemic, two-thirds of US parents said that parenting is harder today than it was twenty years ago, a fact the majority put down to technology. But consider that the next generation of parents may have to deal with something even more challenging: a world lived entirely through an all-encompassing virtual headset. The point is that there are broader and evolving forces at play; tech, economics, the built environment, working culture, changing gender relations, not to mention global pandemics, that are equally as pivotal as the personal in determining the kind of parent you and your peers become.

So if millennial parents find themselves preaching on the amount of sugar in baked beans to the generation for whom it was a household staple, or on the dangers of microplastics to the generation whose toys were laced with lead paint, or calling out racist, body-shaming, or gendered language to a cohort raised on Benny Hill, then this is in part because parenting is the moment when societal shifts become ingrained in the individual; when one generation finally breaks out to align with the next. Each generation of parents feels compelled, quite rightly, to not only learn from past mistakes but to also prepare the child for the world as it is, not as it was. In other words, the generation gap in parenting is real and also the natural order of things.

And in a society where families are smaller and women are having babies later (and therefore find themselves completely divorced from the world of birthing, breastfeeding, education, and being young by the time they have children), it is little wonder that parents have increasingly turned to experts for help. Between 1975 and the nineties, the number of parenting books increased five-fold. For the millennial generation, it's now become a maxim that Google has replaced Grandma. Each cohort of parents seeks out gurus to show them another way and to help them figure out their generational parental identity.

It was in fact the boomers who, as babies, were the first generation exposed to parenting experts. In 1946, Dr Spock's *Common-Sense Book of Baby and Child Care* set the scene for a new style of post-war parenting that rejected the previous belief that children should be seen and not heard and instead prioritised the emotional wellbeing of the individualised child. Out went outdated notions that breastfeeding was animalistic and that babies shouldn't be fed on demand. Dr Spock's advice, leaning heavily on Freudian analysis, was to trust your instincts, shower children with affection, and treat them as individuals. His book would go on to become the third best-selling book of the twentieth century, after Shakespeare and the Bible. Twenty-six pages of advertising accompanied Dr Spock's seminal text, proving there's nothing new in the commercial exploitation of anxious parents.

When boomers became parents, it precipitated a new wave of advice. Heidi Murkoff kicked off in 1984 with *What to Expect When You Are Expecting*, setting in motion a culture of maternal bodily self-regulation and responsibility: out went smoking and in came listening to Mozart to improve the babies' brain function. Boomers were encouraged to be more invested and individualistic in their parenting, with educational attainment the ultimate aspiration. The nineties gave birth to the helicopter mum, always hovering near, monitoring progress and safety in a structured environment. Running parallel was a new fashion for maternal naturalism pioneered by Dr William Sears, whose attachment parenting theory advocated co-sleeping and breast-feeding into toddlerhood. Amid it all, were we getting any closer to raising the perfect generation of kids? No: those experts were merely reflecting the new needs and anxieties of their chief audience, and a growing one at that – the degree-educated working mother.

And today, as millennial parents take the helm, a new consensus and fresh expectations are being forged: parents who see the current mental health crisis in teens and are committed to building emotional resilience in their toddlers; parents who themselves bear the scars from the 'sink or swim' education system and are instead encouraging creativity, play and an acceptance of failure; parents who fear the dependency on screens and fixate on forest school as the antidote. Helicopter parenting is out of fashion, only to be replaced with 'pilot parenting': the idea that parents share in the experience alongside the child, whether it be craft making or watching TV. Today, working mothers spend just as much time with their kids as stay-at-home mothers did in the seventies. This new expectation on 'quality time' is social tyranny – costly in terms of time and money, socially exclusionary, and increasingly impossible in dual-working households during a cost-of-living crisis.

One certainty is that yet another reckoning will come, probably when Generation Alpha enters the workplace and their Gen Z managers are confronted with a workforce they can neither understand nor manage (just as they become parents themselves). It all points to an overarching truth: if company bosses really want to understand how to manage the generations, they would do well to look at the history of parenting – the evolving trends wherein each generation is forged and where the generation gap truly begins. And for those parents and grandparents clashing over parenting styles, I recommend that both seek comfort in the words of Philip Larkin:

This Be The Verse

They fuck you up, your mum and dad.
They may not mean to, but they do.
They fill you with the faults they had
And add some extra, just for you.
But they were fucked up in their turn
By fools in old-style hats and coats,
Who half the time were soppy-stern
And half at one another's throats.

9. Why We Are Living in an Inheritance Economy
(Published: 24 August 2022)

It is hard for any of us to think in terms of billions, let alone trillions, but those are the values we need to use when it comes to the sums around family inheritance. In the UK over the next thirty years, approximately £5.5 trillion of family wealth will be transferred down the generations[147]. In the US, the reported figure ranges from $30-$68 trillion. It will be the largest transference of wealth in human history.

There was a time, not that long ago, when inheritance and all the considerations that come with it was the preserve of the aristocracy – so much so that it formed the narrative backbone of most nineteenth-century novels. And yet in the twenty-first century, inheritance has become democratised; shaping family finances across the class system. As a result, it has also become a prominent thread in this century's story of rising social inequality, intergenerational unfairness, the property and asset bubble, delayed adulthood, and dependency culture within the family.

Whether we realise it or not, we are living in the inheritance economy where, if you are under forty, your life's chances and opportunities are to a large extent determined by what you are set to inherit rather than what you learn or earn. Familial financial support is the defining millennial privilege and the dividing line shaping our past, present, and future.

So how did we get here? More than seventy per cent of household wealth in the UK is held by the over-50s[148] and in the US, the statistic is roughly the same. We know that wealth and assets dominate the economy and that they are uniquely held by older generations. As we are all beginning to appreciate, it's not because that generation worked exceptionally hard but because they were the benefactors of exceptional social, economic, and political conditions unlikely ever to be repeated (sorry, millennials). The post-war combination of good wages, generous pensions, and affordable homes has resulted in the accumulation of wealth in the hands of one demographic across the Western world. And there is a decidedly racial element in this intergenerational unfairness: black millennials in the US, for example, own fifty-two per cent less wealth than black baby boomers had generated by their age[149].

To put it crudely, the circumstances of a meritocratic society have, over time, given rise to a form of generational plutocracy. In the UK, this wealth has not been 'earned' as such, because seventy per cent of it is tied up in property[150], the value of which reflects the UK's short supply rather than owner investment. Forget blaming Thatcher or Reagan – the right or wrongs of this evolution are now largely irrelevant. The important fact is that the boomer generation is dying out and the wealth is on the move.

Where it goes is a question that will directly or indirectly dominate politics for the next twenty years.

In America, it has been estimated that Gen X will inherit fifty-seven per cent of this wealth, while millennials will inherit the rest[151]. In reality though, most of it will come too late for either to spend on themselves, and most likely will be passed on to their Generation Z and Generation Alpha kids respectively. Grandparents are already paying fifteen to twenty per cent of private school fees in the UK. The legacy of what the financial services industry calls the Great Wealth Transfer will continue to impact generations to come.

Millennials on average are set to receive sixteen per cent of their lifetime household income in the form of inheritance[152], which is perhaps why nine out of ten people in the UK say they are relying on a lump sum to pay off debts and subsidise their retirement[153]. Sixty-six per cent of millennials in particular are hopeful that an inheritance will fund their lifestyle and provide the financial security that has so far eluded them[154]. Given this reliance, it is little wonder then that one in five millennials worry that their parents are squandering that inheritance through overspending[155]. And that is before the social care receipts come in.

This culture of reliance, or expectation, has its downsides and is already beginning to play out in the law courts. In the UK High Court, inheritance disputes have tripled in the last decade[156]. With the complexities of the modern blended family, with divorces and stepchildren, that is only set to increase. Alongside the lawyers, legions of financial advisors and wealth managers – sectors built around preserving and growing wealth – are hoping to reap the rewards. In fact, they have been capitalising on the baby boomer buck since the eighties, but they may well find their midlife millennial inheritors will be more predisposed to spending than saving.

Back in the nineties, we still believed that university was the principal driver of opportunity and advancement. I was the first person in my family to get a degree, but that statement tempts a complete misreading of my current class, parental support, and privilege. For the millennial generation, the distinction is not the launch pad of a degree but the safety net of Mum and Dad and whether they were canny enough to buy property in the eighties and nineties.

We know that the Bank of Mum and Dad typically lends £6bn a year, making it the equivalent of a top-ten UK mortgage lender[157]; what is less calculable is the aggregate effect of parental support that affluent millennials were able to tap into as they meandered through early adulthood. There are many who had the luxury of having their inheritance drip-fed to them throughout their twenties and thirties, helping them prolong adolescence and fast-track into adulthood on their own terms.

When millennials were young, we were never naive enough to think that school and university was a level playing field, and yet the real division was only truly revealed at early adulthood, often at the point of graduation. The distinction between those who never received letters from the Student Loans Company and those that still get them in their forties, between those who could afford to pursue more qualifications and those who did not have the luxury of trying out different career options, between those who could seamlessly migrate to a city and those who never left their hometown, between those who received a monthly parental direct debit to supplement their low wages and those who only ever had multiple jobs, between those who received a wedge of a deposit for a first flat and those who will never be able to afford a home, between those who had an all-inclusive wedding and nursery fees paid by grandma and those who've struggled with the traditional load of adult responsibility.

For these reasons, the inheritance economy is not only responsible for much of our current levels of inequality but will also be instrumental in perpetuating it. For the past ten years, the millennial generational identity has crystallised around a compelling narrative of intergenerational unfairness, but this solidarity will come unstuck as their parents die out and the wealth trickles down to the lucky ones. What we are facing is a moment where intergenerational warfare will transition into *intra*generational class conflict. And yet, *class conflict* is not quite the right phrase here: the inheritance economy is also changing the definition of class itself. No longer is your class tied to your professional status or even what you earn; arguably the most frustrated and stunted group comprises those graduates with professional, well-paid jobs who are struggling to maintain the middle-class lifestyle with which their job is traditionally associated; academics being the obvious example. And they are the lucky ones. Those non-graduates with limited access to professional, well-paid jobs and little inheritance are the ones targeted by the UK's levelling up agenda precisely because they have been forgotten for so long.

Where all this goes politically is the key question. Jeremy Corbyn's appeal was precisely to the frustrated urban-dwelling/graduate professional/millennial demographic even though his pledge to raise inheritance tax in his 2019 manifesto was still moderate compared to historical standards in the UK. Few politicians would dare take French economist Thomas Piketty's line that private property should be temporary and that you shouldn't be allowed to pass it on when you die. Any government, right or left, pledging a redistributive policy to even out the playing field (either on inheritance tax or capital gains tax regarding property) runs the serious risk of alienating boomers who want to help their kids and the more hard-headed millennials who expect to inherit. It will be a tricky balancing act. The inheritance economy produces a fundamental problem for politicians and arguably democracy itself, where any promises of making life better for the next generation ultimately ring hollow against a system of insurmountable unfairness.

Ultimately, the inheritance economy will prove deeply problematic for us all: for employers who find it hard to motivate their employees through salary alone; for families seeking to navigate the transference as elegantly and as painlessly as possible in the context of an ageing society; and especially for millennials, because we were the generation who were told that if you worked hard and were martyrs to the philosophy of self-improvement and self-actualisation, then you could achieve anything. The truth is that our fate was always tied to our parents' purses. It's trickle-down economics but not as we know it, and the consequences will be profound.

Acknowledgements

Writing requires time and space - both physical and mental. Firstly, huge thanks go to Emma Fagg, my brilliant researcher who always manages to source the right material with speed and accuracy. Thanks, also, to Matilda Wanless for giving Penguin a run for their money on the cover design, and Christina Wooderson, my brilliant PA and guardian of my time - without whom I would not function.

A great deal of thanks must go to all the companies, organisations, and government bodies that have opened their doors and invited me to share my research and ideas with them, but which in turn have shared their concerns, triumphs and difficulties when it comes to how their workforce, consumer and society is at large changing. And immeasurable thanks go to Katy Cole and the Spoken team for facilitating and engineering all these connections.

Finally, thank you to my family; my husband Christian and our two children Chaplin and Amaryllis. For two years I was caught in a multi-generational household, living with my mother as well as my young kids. It was tough, but it also inspired a lot of these ideas and conversations. (Having said that, Christian, you are a saint for putting up with the situation for as long as you did!)

About the Author

Dr Eliza Filby is a writer, speaker, and consultant who specialises in 'generational intelligence', helping companies, governments, and services understand generational shifts within politics, society, and the workplace.

Eliza has worked with a variety of organisations, from VICE Media to Warner Brothers, from the UK's Ministry of Defence and the Bank of England to the Royal Household, and with banks such as HSBC, Barclays, and BNY Mellon. She has spoken at the EU's Human Rights Forum on teenagers and technology, to the EU Commission on the future of work and to the UK's House of Lords Select Committee on Intergenerational Unfairness. She currently sits on the board of the Mission Group plc. as a non-executive director.

In 2022 she was awarded the Europa Forum's 2022 Millennial Leaders Award for her work on generational change. Eliza is the author of *God and Mrs Thatcher: The Battle for Britain's Soul* as well as several reports, from *Fuelling Gender Diversity: Unlocking the Next Generation Workplace* and *Mind the Gap: Managing a Multi-Generational Workforce in the Post Pandemic Age.* She runs her own course library specialising on generational intelligence with respect to the workplace and the Great Wealth Transfer.

She also hosts her own podcast on the generation gap, *It's All Relative*, and can be found on TikTok *trying* to communicate with Gen Z.

Eliza received her PhD from the University of Warwick and subsequently taught at King's College, London and at the University of Renmin in China. Her writing has been published in *The Times, The Guardian,* the *New Statesman* and the *Financial Times.*

Her work can be found on her website www.elizafilby.com and you find out more @drelizafilby on Instagram, LinkedIn, TikTok, and Twitter.

She lives in London with her husband and her two children.

Endnotes

1 State of the Global Workplace survey, Gallup, 2017

2 Harriet Hall, Goldman Sachs's egg-freezing scheme is a pathway to a hellish dystopia, The Independent, 5 November 2019

3 Emily Canal, High-Tech Cribs, Breast Milk Delivery, and Traveling Nannies: Just Some of the Perks Companies Are Offering New Parents Inc, 7 February 2019

4 Maureen Farrell, Liz Hoffman, Eliot Brown and David Benoit, The Fall of WeWork: How a Startup Darling Came Unglued, The Wall Street Journal, 24 October 2019

5 Need to Form a New Habit? Give Yourself At Least 66 Days, PsychCentral

6 Large majority of Britons predict coronavirus will lead to changes in our lives, work, economy and society even one year from now – but expect less changes to the way we are governed, Ipsos MORI, 7 May 2020

7 Professor Keith Willison and Matthew Lesh, Shifting Out Of Lockdown: The Four Days On, Ten Days Off Model, The Adam Smith Institute, 6 May 2020

8 Coronavirus and the latest indicators for the UK economy and society, Office for National Statistics, 18 June 2020

9 U.S. Bureau of Labor Statistic, June 2020

10 OECD, March – May 2020

11 NGO Global Action Plan and Business for Clean Air Taskforce Survey, June 2020

12 GDP monthly estimate, UK: May 2020, Office for National Statistics, 14 July 2020

13 Steve Crabtree, Worldwide, 13% of Employees Are Engaged at Work, Gallup, 8 October 2013

14 Embracing the Age of Ambiguity', Aviva, November 2020

15 Mark Bridge, Ditch the shirt – your next office will be a clubhouse, The Times, 24 June 2020

16 Joshua Murray-Nevill, Lockdown loneliness strikes UK workers, Total Jobs, 17 August 2020

17 Professor Keith Willison and Matthew Lesh, Shifting Out of Lockdown: The Four Days On, Ten Days Off Approach, Adam Smith Institute, 6 May 2020

18 Business and individual attitudes towards the future of homeworking, UK: April to May 2021, Office for National Statistics, 14 June 2021

19 Michiel Willems, Half of all employed women in UK reconsidering career options post-pandemic, City A.M., 14 July 2021

20 Richard Partington, London population set to decline for first time since 1988 – report, The Guardian, 7 January 2021

21 The Modern Families Index 2018

22 Jess Huang, Alexis Krivkovich, Ishanaa Rambachan, and Lareina Yee, For mothers in the workplace, a year (and counting) like no other, McKinsey & Company, 5 May 2021

23 How Have Living Arrangements and Marital Status in England and Wales Changed Since 2001?, Office for National Statistics, 27 March 2014

24 Olivia Rockeman, Americans Are Done With 5-Days a Week in the Office. Here's What That Means for the Economy, Bloomberg, 1 June 2021

25 Business and individual attitudes towards the future of homeworking, UK: April to May 2021, Office for National Statistics, 14 June 2021

26 Avivah Wittenberg-Cox, If You Can't Find a Spouse Who Supports Your Career, Stay Single, Harvard Business Review, 24 October 2017

27 Lucy Tobin, 'Grunts' on £150,000 a year: inside the war for London's legal talent, Evening Standard, 28 January 2022

28 30% Club Study, March 2014

29 Marla Tabaka, 9 CEOs Share How Being a Dad Has Made Them Better Leaders, Inc, 9 June 2016

30 M.S. Dahl., C.L. Dezső,, & D.G. Ross, D. G., Fatherhood and Managerial Style: How a Male CEO's Children Affect the Wages of His Employees*. Administrative Science Quarterly, 57(4), 669–693, 2012

31 Sylvia Ann Hewlett, Executive Women and the Myth of Having It All, Harvard Business Review, April 2002

[32] Moms, Work and the Pandemic, US Census Bureau, March 2021

[33] The Primal Scream Line (212-556-3800), The New York Times, 2020

34 Simon Sinek, Leaders Eat Last, Portfolio, 2014

35 ONS, Employment in the UK: September 2022

36 Pregnant Than Screwed and Mumsnet Survey, March 2022

37 Victoria Benson, CEO of single mother charity: Gingerbread, June 2022

38 Harriet Olorenshaw and Christine Farquharson, The changing cost of childcare, IFS, 20 May 2022

39 Pregnant Than Screwed and Mumsnet Survey, March 2022

40 Early Years Alliance Survey, March 2022

41 Pregnant Than Screwed and Mumsnet Survey, March 2022

42 Care.com Cost of Care Survey, June 2022

43 Tom Calver, Held back: the mothers who can't afford to return to work, The Sunday Times, 5 June 2022

44 Alicia Sasser Modestino, Jamie J. Ladge, Addie Swartz, and Alisa Lincoln, Childcare Is a Business Issue, Harvard Business Review, 29 April 2021

45 The Modern Families Index, 2018

46 Net childcare costs, OECD, 2021

47 Gina Chon, Companies offering child care get grown-up payback, Reuters, 20 August 2021

48 Child Care Plus®, Bank of America

49 Camila Beiner, Child care is getting more support from some private companies, NPR, 4 January 2022

50 Beamery Talent Index: Third Edition, January 2022

51 Beamery Talent Index: Third Edition, January 2022

52 Jean M. Twenge, Have Smartphones Destroyed A Generation?, The Atlantic, September 2017

53 What Americans think about the Economy, AP-NORC at the University of Chicago, February 2018

54 The Cambridge Analytica Files, The Guardian, March 2018

55 Halifax Pocket Money Survey

56 Shingi Mararike, Sexting is better than the real thing for Generation Sensible, The Times, 16 September 2018

57 Adult drinking habits in Great Britain: 2005 to 2016, Office for National Statistics, 3 May 2017

58 Rosemary Bennett, Parents post 1,500 pictures of children on social media before fifth birthday, The Times, 6 September 2016

59 Smartphone Screen Time: Baby Boomers and Millennials, Provision Living, 1 March 2019

60 Reaching Today's Boomers & Seniors Online, Google and Ipsos, 2013

61 Social Media Matters for Baby Boomers, Forbes, 6 March 2018

62 Niall McCarthy, Is Facebook Becoming Social Media's Retirement Home?, Forbes, 8 March 2019

63 Digital graveyards: are the dead taking over Facebook?, University of Oxford, 29 April 2019

64 Facebook Motivations Study: Why We Share, Fractl, April 2016

65 Andrew Guess, Jonathan Nagler and Joshua Tucker, Less than you think: Prevalence and predictors of fake news dissemination on Facebook, Science Advances, 9 January 2019

66 Centre for Economics and Business Research (CEBR), 2020

67 Passing on the Pounds: the rise of the UK's inheritance economy, Kings Court Trust, 2017

68 Pooneh Baghai, Olivia Howard, Lakshmi Prakash and Jill Zucker, Women as the next wave of growth in US wealth management, McKinsey, 29 July 2020

69 New York Life Survey, 2020

70 YouGov Poll for Age UK, 2017

71 ONS, 2014

72 Ludlowthompson, 2020

73 The Insolvency Service, 2020

74 Barclays, 2017

75 U.S. Government Consumer Expenditure Survey and Neilson, 2018

76 Richard Fry, Millennials overtake Baby Boomers as America's largest generation, Pew Research Center, 28 April 2020

77 Distribution of Household Wealth in the U.S., Federal Reserve Board, Q2:2022

78 Liabilities per Generation, Federal Reserve Board, Q2:2022

79 The Bank of Mum and Dad, Legal & General, 2021

80 ONS, 2014

81 The Transamerica Center for Retirement Studies (TCRS), 2019

82 Report: The forgotten generation? International Longevity
Centre – UK, March 2021

83 Longevity and the New Journey of Retirement, Edward Jones
and Age Wave, 2022

84 Report: The forgotten generation? International Longevity
Centre – UK, March 2021

85 Nearly One in Two (46%) of the Entire Self Employed
Workforce in the UK is now Over the Age of 50 Rest Less, 26 July
2019

86 UCL Centre for Longitudinal Studies, 2020

87 UCL Centre for Longitudinal Studies, 2020

88 Q1 2021 Automotive Market Trends Review, Experian

89 Generation Z Turning To Buy Now Pay Later Schemes To Fund
Spending During Lockdown, comparethemarket.com, 2 June 2020

90 Sam Meadows and Anna Mikhailova, Lockdown pays off for
two million high-earning households, The Telegraph, 9 June 2020

91 Adam Williams, Buy now, debt later: how the lure of Klarna
encourages young people to spend, The Telegraph, 8 February 2020

92 Adam Williams, Buy now, debt later: how the lure of Klarna
encourages young people to spend, The Telegraph, 8 February 2020

93 Lucy Burton, Big banks struggling to cater for clued up
Generation Z's needs, The Telegraph, 25 February 2018

94 Kate Palmer, Younger adults prefer saving to spending, The
Times, 14 April 2019

95 Edoardo Moreno, Emma launches Monzo integration, Emma, 22
January 2018

96 Laura Miller, Easy credit, hard times: 10-fold rise in young
people going bankrupt, The Telegraph, 30 July 2019

97 Harriet Russell, Gen Z is paying the price for quick and cheap
debt, The Telegraph, 12 May 2019

98 One in five young people use a credit card everyday, Credit
Connect, 17 September 2019

99 Alice Hancock, UK restaurants warn social distancing will put
them out of business, Financial Times, 1 May 2020

100 Alice Hancock, UK restaurants warn social distancing will put
them out of business, Financial Times, 1 May 2020

101 Having a haircut and popping to the pub: Millennials' post-
lockdown priorities revealed, Barclays, 18 May 2020

102 Money Talks: Behavioural Impact of COVID 19, Ipsos Mori 24 April 2020

103 Having a haircut and popping to the pub: Millennials' post-lockdown priorities revealed, Barclays, 18 May 2020

104 Stephen Hayward, Coronavirus could see package holiday prices double due to social distancing on planes, The Mirror, 16 May 2020

105 Airbnb to axe 25% of workforce, The Financial Times, 5 May 2020

106 Jack Maidment, Ashley Kirk, Charlotte Krol, and Aaron Wheeler, Why Jeremy Corbyn's 2017 general election 'youthquake' was a 'myth', The Telegraph, 2 February 2018

107 Ipsos MORI Thinks: Millennial Myths and Realities, May 2017

108 YouGov, May 2017

109 The new University Challenge: Justify top fees as only half of graduates get graduate-level jobs, CIPD, 16 November 2017

110 Office for National Statistics, 2017

111 Babies in Lockdown, Parent Infant Foundation, August 2020

112 Perri Klass, Do Masks Impede Children's Development?, The New York Times, 14 September 2020

113 UK lockdown linked to widening disadvantage gap for babies and toddlers, Oxford Brookes University, 27 October 2020

114 Elena Magrini, How will Coronavirus affect jobs in different parts of the country?, Centre for Cities, 17 March 2020

115 Isolated and Struggling: Social isolation and the risk of child abuse during and after the coronavirus pandemic, NSPCC Learning, June 2020

116 Chris Smyth and Rosemary Bennett, Don't kill granny with coronavirus, warns Matt Hancock, The Times, 8 September 2020

117 Amelia Hill, How the UK halved its teenage pregnancy rate, The Guardian, 18 July 2016

118 Divorces in England and Wales: 2017, Office for National Statistics, 26 September 2018

119 Shireen Kanji, Grandparent Care: A Key Factor in Mothers' Labour Force Participation in the UK, Cambridge University Press, 7 November 2017

120 Lizzie Thomson, Grandparents save UK parents more than £16 billion a year with childcare, Metro, 25 September 2020

121 1 in 3 homes are multi-generational, Aviva, 11 September 2020
122 1 in 3 homes are multi-generational, Aviva, 11 September 2020
123 Covid-19 mortality highly influenced by age demographics, University of Oxford, 17 April 2020
124 Unpaid carers provide social care worth £57 billion, Office for National Statistics, 10 July 2017
125 A fifth of over-45s expect to leave work to become carers, Financial Times, 10 October 2019
126 Two-thirds of young Italians are still living with their parents, The Local, 18 December 2018
127 Divorces in England and Wales: 2017, Office for National Statistics, 26 September 2018
128 Parents now spend twice as much time with their children as 50 years ago, The Economist, 27 November 2017
129 Beth Greenfield, Same-Sex Parents Spend More Time With Kids, Study Finds, Yahoo! News, 19 October 2015
130 Parents Expect Their Children To Become Financial Grown-ups At The Age Of 29, Sainsbury's, 19 September 2016
131 Christina Hall, #BIYP: An Opportunity to Say Thanks for Everything They've Taught You, LinkedIn Official Blog, 16 November 2018
132 Tom Jenkin, Word to your mother: A quarter of girls take their mum out clubbing, The Tab, 16 March 2015
133 Phil Davies, First Choice research reveals rise in multi-generational holidays, Travel Weekly, 12 June 2019
134 Isabelle Fraser, Bank of Mum and Dad now equivalent to the ninth biggest mortgage lender, paying out £6.5bn, The Telegraph, 2 May 2017
135 Employed graduates in non-graduate roles, parts of the UK, 2015 to 2019, Office for National Statistics, 16 November 2020
136 Chinese university graduates rise exponentially, have diverse career options, China Daily, 24 June 2019
137 State of Working India, Centre for Sustainable Employment of the Azim Premji University, 2018
138 Penguin Random House scraps degree requirement for future workers, The Telegraph, 18 January 2016
139 Sean Coughlan, Two degrees now needed to get higher pay, BBC News, 26 April 2019

140 The New Work Order, Foundation for Young Australians, 2017
141 Robert Lindsay, Many Rebels of the 1960's Depressed as They Near 30, The New York Times, 29 February 1976
142 Chris Weller, This 40 year study shows us what's different about Gen Z, World Economic Forum, 27 September 2017
143 David Lewis, Bereaved push for greater access to loved ones' social media, email accounts, ABC News, 6 January 2015
144 Digital graveyard: are the dead taking over Facebook?, Oxford University Institute, 29 April 2019
145 Samantha Hissong, Would You Pay To Be 'Buried' in a Metaverse Cemetery?, 11 December 2021
146 Minwoo Park, South Korean mother given tearful VR reunion with deceased daughter, Reuters, 14 February 2020
147 Passing on the Pounds, Kings Court Trust, 2017
148 Over 50s contribute more than 6 trillion to the UK economy, Saga Investment Services, 22 January 2016
149 Disparities by Race, Ethnicity and Education Underlie Millennials' Comeback in Wealth, The Federal Reserve Bank of St Louis, 1 April 2021
150 The Centre for Economic and Business Research & Kings Court Trust, 2017
151 Cerulli Associates, 2019
152 Pascale Bourquin, Robert Joyce and David Sturrock, Inheritances and inequality over the life cycle: what will they mean for younger generations?, Institute for Fiscal Studies, April 2021
153 The 'I' Word, Tower Street Finance, 2021
154 First Direct, March 2018
155 First Direct, March 2018
156 Inheritance disputes rise as families go to war over estates, Financial Times, 16 July 2020
157 The Bank of Mum and Dad, Legal & General, 2021